Understanding Motivation for Lifelong Learning

by Jim Smith and Andrea Spurling

CAMPAIGN
FOR **LEARNING**

NIACE

THE NATIONAL ORGANISATION
FOR ADULT LEARNING

Dedication:

To our parents, with love and gratitude:

Estelle and Arthur Farrow

Freda Molly and Rowland Smith

Copyright © Text Campaign for Learning

First published in 2001 by the
Campaign for Learning
19, Buckingham Street
London WC2N 6EF
www.campaign-for-learning.org.uk

NIACE: www.niace.org.uk

Produced for the Campaign for Learning by
Southgate Publishers
The Square
Sandford
Nr Crediton
Devon EX17 4LW

Printed and bound in Great Britain by Short Run Press, Exeter, Devon

British Library Cataloguing in Publication Data
A CIP catalogue record for this book is available from the British Library

ISBN 1 903107 00 8

Contents

Foreword   Page iv

Preface   Page v

Chapter 1: **Motivation to learn**   Page 1

Chapter 2: **Different faces of learning motivation**   Page 7

Chapter 3: **Motivation for learning activity**   Page 18

Chapter 4: **Motivation for learning strategy**   Page 38

Chapter 5: **Developing learning motivation in the family** Page 49

Chapter 6: **The family's wider influence on motivation**   Page 65

Chapter 7: **Other influential environments**   Page 78

Chapter 8: **Policy implications**   Page 100

Postscript: **Agenda for action**   Page 116

References   Page 121

Foreword

Bill Lucas, Chief Executive, Campaign for Learning

ONE OF THE SPECIAL THINGS ABOUT learning is that nobody can make you do it.

As a child, you can be taken to a school and play intellectual truant through all of your classes. Or, as an adult, you can be sent on a training course but refuse to absorb what you are offered. And you can resolutely resist taking an active part in DIY of any kind!

For the last five years, the Campaign for Learning has been seeking to understand the complex issue of motivation. We now, for example, know a lot more about what may turn particular people on to learning and we can anticipate some of the things which will switch people off. It is clear that we are all born with an appetite to learn but that, in a matter of a few years, our taste for it can become soured. It is also clear to us that everyone has the capacity to learn and to recover their hunger for learning, however de-motivated they may have become.

Above all we have become acutely aware that motivation to learn is quite different from motivation to do other things in life; for our sense of self-worth and view of our personality are intimately involved in our learning.

As we find out more about how our minds work, we have found out more about the kind of activity that needs to take place before and after any episode of learning. This study of motivation explores the factors which go into determining whether we are ready or not to learn. It focuses mainly on what happens before learning although, as the authors make clear, sustained motivation is also connected with our experiences of learning and the degree to which we consider ourselves to be successful as learners.

Jim Smith and Andrea Spurling have a deservedly high reputation for the quality of their thinking about lifelong learning. In this book they present a broad overview of current thinking. But they have gone further than this by seeking to outline policy implications and move towards a national strategy. In partnership with NIACE, we are delighted to be able to help initiate a serious public debate about this important topic.

As Jim and Andrea are well aware, I do not agree with all of the conclusions they draw from their research and from the workshops with practitioners which I was pleased to be able to facilitate. But I am absolutely at one with them in seeing the issue of motivation as being central to fulfilling any vision of a learning society.

We all hope that this book will stimulate ideas and fresh thinking among policy-makers and learning providers of all kinds, making an understanding of motivation to learn a vital part of our approach.

Bill Lucas

Preface

THIS BOOK IS AN OVERVIEW OF CONTEMPO-
rary thinking on the motivation for
lifelong learning. It brings together the
wide ranging and fragmented literature on
motivation to learn, as it runs across the
boundaries of psychology, sociology,
anthropology, economics, and the study of
learning itself. It is the product of an
18 month study funded by the Esmée
Fairbairn Foundation and the Talent
Foundation, and supported by the Campaign
for Learning, combining desk research,
interviews and workshops. A parallel
project, supported by the University for
Industry, provided valuable insight into the
prospect for effective surveys of motivation
to learn.

The study was undertaken in four stages.
The first three stages covered motivation
for work-related learning, community-
related learning, and individual and family-
based learning, respectively. Reports have
been produced and published on each.
Seminars on the second and third stages
involved experts and practitioners to dis-
cuss and emend the material in the reports.
Further details are on our web site
www.bamfordtaggs.co.uk

In the fourth and final stage, the material in
the three stage reports has been brought
together and extended into a single statement covering the whole field. This is set
out in the eight chapters which follow. The
book refers to the motivation both for individual learning projects and for learning
strategies which people pursue over
extended periods.

Chapters 1, 2, 3 and 4 contain an eclectic
theory of individual motivation to learn. This
aims to draw a coherent picture in clear and
simple terms, as uncluttered as possible by
academic and technical jargon.

Chapters 5, 6 and 7 contain a systematic
discussion of the forces which shape motivation to learn, by attaching themselves to
the external leverage points which the theory of individual motivation provides.

Chapter 8 contains a first attempt to set out
a motivational strategy which will help to
shift the UK towards a culture of lifelong
learning.

The final chapter is an Agenda for Action to
accompany the strategy.

Running through these chapters are a
number of concerns. Firstly, it seemed to us
important to be prepared to take a number
of risks in order to put together a reasonably complete picture, if only for other
people to engage with. As far as we know,
no similar overview is currently available,
at any level of sophistication.

Secondly, it would have been only too easy
to shrink from this work of assembly as
soon as direct evidence runs thin. Such are

the gaps and inconsistencies in the literature and the data, that we have often had to carry across evidence from other fields of motivation into the learning domain. We believe that the picture we have drawn is robust, but here and there the ice is thin. We hope that this work will encourage others to bring forward new evidence, to extend or consolidate our account.

Thirdly, it seemed important to ignore academic boundaries on this occasion. There is a long history of different disciplines trying to capture the motivational issue for themselves alone, and this is largely the reason why the study of motivation to learn has not prospered. What we offer here is an integrated approach, putting the best human capital theories from economists together with theories from sociologists, psychologists, social psychologists and others.

Fourthly, we intended that the picture of motivation presented here should include the spiritual-aesthetic dimension, along with cultural and materialistic aims. We have made steps towards this, but further work still needs to be carried out to develop this spiritual theme fully, and link it to concerns with moral thinking and creativity.

Finally, our purpose has been to complement the work we have undertaken in recent years on the development of a culture of cradle-to-grave lifelong learning for the UK. This is set out in our book *Lifelong Learning: Riding the Tiger*, published in 1999 by Cassell, with support from the Lifelong Learning Foundation. This showed what a lifelong learning culture would be like, and what practical steps might move towards it. But there remained the key question "What would have to be done to lead people to really want to participate in such a culture?" We believe that in these chapters the first intimations of an answer to that question can be seen. In current social and economic conditions it will not be easy, but it is certainly not impossible.

Acknowledgements

We are indebted to the Esmée Fairbairn Foundation and the Talent Foundation for enabling this work to be done, and to the Campaign for Learning and its sponsors for their valuable support for the work itself, the seminars, and now the final publication. We have also benefited greatly from the involvement of people who shared their experience with us in workshops, and others who gave their time for interview. This book would not have been the same without their help, and we thank them all. Responsibility for the views expressed, however, is ours alone.

Jim Smith and Andrea Spurling
www.bamfordtaggs.co.uk

March 2001

Chapter 1:
Motivation to learn

Introduction

This book offers a new way of thinking about people's motivation to learn. It brings together in an accessible form recent motivation research from psychology, sociology and economics, undertaken in Britain and elsewhere. First it sets the many conceptual strands into a common framework; then it examines how motivation to learn can be influenced; and finally it introduces a long term motivation strategy which could help to develop a lifelong learning society for the UK.

Motivation to learn is an urgent issue politically, economically and socially, yet it has been sadly neglected. As a subject of study it is divided across several academic disciplines, and little synthesis has been undertaken. There has also been a tendency to assume that the nub of the subject lies with children at school, so that the motivation of adults in the field of learning has been examined less closely. This book aims therefore to integrate the many academic strands, and to take a lifelong perspective in doing so. The fragmentation of knowledge about motivation has inhibited the development of clear, effective motivation policies and strategies, at all organisational levels. A new comprehensive view of motivation is needed if progress is to be made on policy and good practice.

We have written this book for two reasons. Firstly, to lay to rest the ghost of an old

doctrine, which held that motivation to learn was an in-built property, possessed by the best people and not by all the rest. Research evidence shows that such self-justificatory beliefs are well past their use-by date. Secondly, because our work over the last five years shows that a genuine culture change in policy and practice is needed to establish lifelong learning in the UK over the next twenty years or so; and a strong motivation for learning among people of all ages is a fundamental part of such a change.

On the basis of the material reviewed here, our fundamental assertions are these:

1. The levels of learning motivation displayed by individuals reflect their social and economic experience in general, and their family experience in particular.[1]

2. Despite this experience every healthy person can, in principle, rise to high levels of motivation to learn. It may be hard, but people are not condemned to low motivation by their genes, or position in life. Good motivation to learn, like other resources, can, and should, be spread more widely.

3. At every point in our society, practical steps can be taken to improve learning motivation significantly. These need to be brought together into a long term motivational strategy.[2]

What is motivation?

This enquiry needs a clear definition of motivation. Most of the relevant research treats it as the personal experience of keenness for pursuing an intended action or goal. The experience is known directly only to the individual who has the motivation. Other people have to recognise its existence from what that individual says and does, and the emotions he or she displays. People are generally quite skilled at doing this.

This keenness is the product of a private mental process, during which individuals weigh up the pros and cons of a potential action or goal, and assess the likely personal benefits and costs.[3] Whether they do the assessment entirely in the head, or work it out in written notes or in conversations with other people does not really matter. Research shows that if the elements in this internal appraisal are changed, the levels of keenness experienced by individuals will also change in broadly predictable ways. This is the motivation process at work.[4]

This book looks at how internal appraisal works in the case of learning. The broad structure of the motivation process is more or less the same for everyone, but individuals differ in the detail of how they apply it. The effort and time they put into assessment varies; and the beliefs and information, which are the inputs, are tailored by individuals' specific experiences. Each individual will therefore have a personal motivation system with precise settings which are unique (rather as standard software programs can be individualised).

It is tempting to see keenness as a form of energy, pumped up by the motivation system until it bursts into action. Motivation would not, however, be any old bang, going off in random directions. Its extraordinary potency comes from being purposeful, focused on a particular action or goal. When the stored energy is released it discharges in a given direction, like action in a wound-up spring.[5] The effect can move people bodily – from the couch to their feet; from kitchen to college; from one part of the globe to another.

People who say they feel motivated for something in particular tend to act in predictable ways: they have a strong preference for their intended action, and against the attraction of alternatives; they show persistence, focus, and resilience in its favour; and they make strong efforts to complete the action. The higher their motivation, the more marked these consequences are. For example, the person who really, really wants to learn how to swim can even overcome a terror of drowning.

In real life, motivation is not just a person's keenness for something ; it always favours that action or goal against some perceived alternative(s). Such alternatives will sometimes be clearly perceived, sometimes not. They can include various things avoided, or done without – or they may simply be doing nothing out of the ordinary.[6] Motivation is always relative to an alternative or alternatives which have been, or which can be, rejected.

This means that an action or goal has no inherent ability to motivate – it is the context that makes the difference. The possibility of landing a £50,000 job, for example, is likely to be motivating if the alternative is unemployment. But if the alternative is a £150,000 job, motivation for the £50,000 option will be weaker, other things being equal.

What motivation is not

There are a number of common misconceptions which cloud understanding of the motivation process.

- **People who have stronger motivation than others have it because they are more emotional than the others**. Motivation is not itself an emotion.[7] It involves a process engaging both rational and emotional systems in the brain, producing energy for action. Somebody can have strong motivation to learn a new skill (how to drive, or how to play a musical instrument, for example) while being quite dispassionate about it, and without it being a fundamental need or even a profound desire. In fact, if motivation is well-supported it can overcome strong emotions rooted in experience, such as antagonism to learning.

- **Some people have stronger motivation than others, because they have bigger appetites than others**. Motivation does not consist of animal instincts or urges, although such states link up with it in very important ways.[8] It is a cognitive process – a matter of personal perception and assessment related to awareness, to values, and to judgement – but one which is influenced to an extent by feelings and instincts.

- **Some people by their nature have stronger motivation than others, just as some can run faster than others**. Motivation is not purely or inescapably a product of the genes. A great deal of mischief has been done by the notion that motivation is a fixed entity, trait or capacity in a person's character or brain – something like the inherent horsepower of a car, or the capacity of a computer hard disk.[9]

Quantities of research show that motivation is highly malleable. Just as it can be easily damaged and undermined, it can also be restored and grown; engineered and refined; supported and raised.[10]

- **Some people have good reasons for doing some learning, so they must be motivated**. Having motivation as defined here is not the same as having a motive for doing something.[11] Needing a haircut, for example, provides a motive/reason for going to the hairdresser; but if you do not like having your hair cut, even having a motive may not provide the motivation to make you submit to the clippers. Having a reason can influence the process which forms motivation, but it says nothing about the intensity of the keenness itself.

- **Motivation is the process of applying sticks and carrots to others to get them to act as you want them to**. This defines motivation as the activity of giving a spur to other people's action. This is a familiar, and perfectly sensible, use of the term, but it is too narrow to use here. Later chapters will show how such spurring on by employers and others can be highly relevant to the motivation process as defined above.

Identifying motivation to learn

Examining motivation to learn in terms of felt energy requires:
- clarification of the kinds of learning to which the motivation attaches;
- the felt energy being sufficiently measurable to make policy discussion possible.

Definition of learning

We adopt a broad approach to the definition of learning. Only tacit or implicit learning is omitted, on the grounds that it is below the threshold of awareness and intention, and so felt energy does not arise.[12] There are three elements to the definition:

* learning is taken to be a process of acquiring knowledge or skill which adds significantly to the learner's understanding or experience of life.[13] It is not just about managing purely functional information, such as memorising telephone numbers or PIN numbers;
* the relevant learning in this sense including any formal and informal learning which people undertake intentionally, and which they are conscious of receiving;
* it also includes any learning meeting the two conditions above which is:
  * undertaken at any age;
  * supplied by all kinds of supplier, including self-supply;
  * dependent on all kinds of technology from formal class room to the Internet, including learning by doing (and even reading in bed);
  * financed by all kinds of funding bodies or buyers.

Measuring motivation

In this wide field of learning policy-makers need at the very least to know that motivational changes can be identified and monitored reasonably reliably in response to policy changes. The snag is that motivation is a subjective experience, which is private in nature and difficult to express on a numerical scale both for individuals and for groups. It would be nice to know that an individual's learning motivation had changed by x%; and it would be useful to know that the average motivation score for a group of people had shifted by y%. But such precision is not readily available to us. As far as we know there is no direct way of measurement akin to using a thermometer to measure

temperature. There are some physiological measures of arousal, but these do not measure motivation, nor stand as a proxy measure for it.

There has been some use of measures of effort or participation in learning as proxy indicators. But these have only served to obscure the motivational issues. If, for example, the aim is to promote participation in learning by stronger motivation, it does not help if the measure of motivation is provided by the selfsame participation. While it is true that motivated people will tend to make an effort and participate, the reverse is not always true – indeed it is often false. People who participate or make learning effort may be forced to do so; or they may be taking a second best route, which may be better than nothing but less than ideal, involving a mixture of motivation and demotivation. It looks as if all the obvious proxy measures are inadequate.

What can be done is to ask people to indicate the intensity of their keenness for something on a banded (non-numerical) scale, with bands ranging from zero at one end to high at the other. Motivational changes can also be monitored in the same terms. These are ordered scales, which lead to statistics on the proportion of respondents whose self-reported keenness falls into each band. These can be very useful to policy-makers, and do allow for a broad brush approach to before and after monitoring. They do not, however, establish the comparative intensity of the different bands – that a high is x times the intensity of a low, for example, even for the same person, and they do not allow precise comparison between people.

Additional precision can be sought by other means. For example, people could be asked to give a whole set of answers on different banded scales, with their answers coded numerically (1 to 5, say, according to band), and then averaged into a composite numerical score. This is often done by psychologists, but does not really overcome the inherent problems of the use of banded scales. Alternatively, people can be asked to assess changes in motivation on a banded scale, with positive and negative bands. Or, more adventurously, the economists' approach of measuring compensating or equivalent variations could be attempted.[14] These economic techniques rely on asking people what sum of money would induce them to give up the action if they were actively engaged in it, or would give them equivalent satisfaction if they were banned from taking it up in the first place.

Whether it is worth straining for such additional sophistication in measurement depends on the context. The key point is that, with very few exceptions, something useful and good enough can nearly always be done. Many similar problems of measurement are found in the area of consumer tastes and preferences, where the market research industry has been able to get a good purchase on the technical issues involved. Much the same can be done in the area of motivation to learn, where there is a real opportunity for better use of motivation surveys. No one can say that motivation is so inherently unmeasurable that all policy debate has to be cancelled.

Motivation and demotivation

So much for motivation. But what of demotivation? There are two senses of demotivation. The first simply refers to loss of motivation. If a learner's motivational assessment changes, and motivation for any chosen learning is less than it was, the person can be said to be demotivated. This raises no new issues. The second, more interesting, sense is where a person has negative motivation for something which is necessary or enforced.[15] Here Figure 1.1 shows how a positive banded scale can be used to record individuals' perceived motivational energy, if they feel energy towards an intended goal, to the point that – circumstances permitting – they will seek to implement it. If, on the other hand, they prefer the alternative goal, but have to pursue the stipulated goal against their inclination, motivation can be measured negatively as

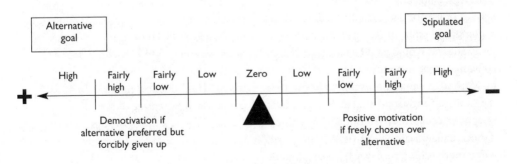

Figure 1.1 Banded scale measuring motivation

demotivation, again using a banded scale. (It is in fact the reverse of motivation which the individuals would have for the alternative over the stipulated goal.) The story of Geri illustrates this point.

> Geri was offered the choice of having money for driving lessons, or having money for a weekend in Paris with her friends, as an 18th birthday present. She had to trade off the attraction of being able to do one against her reluctance (demotivation) in not being able to do the other (both of which would register on a zero-to-high banded scale). In this case, the attraction of driving lessons outweighed her regret over missing a trip to Paris. As a result, she felt positive motivation to get on with the lessons. But if some other learning had been enforced in this case, against a natural preference for the trip to Paris with friends, her reluctance (demotivation) would have registered as a negative score.

Notes and references (Numbers refer to publications listed in the Reference section)

[1] The best sustained account of this proposition is in 9.

[2] See Postscript.

[3] See 193 for a good discussion of this process related definition.

[4] For good short accounts see 174, 193, 229, 241 & 247.

[5] See Lewin in 164 for the 'spring' analogy.

[6] Economists call this the 'do nothing option' and frequently use it as a base for comparing investment options.

[7] The full role of emotion in motivation is still unclear. Emotion is now under close study, after a long period of neglect.

[8] Maslow's theory of motivation envisages a ladder of motivation starting with these instincts. Still popular, it has lacked supporting evidence and is now long superseded. See 168 & 238.

[9] See 69 on a devastating attack on entity beliefs.

[10] See Bandura in 9 & 11.

[11] Many surveys of motivation are in fact surveys of reasons, not energy levels. See 65.

[12] See important work by Eraut in 79; Eraut et al in 80, 81; and by Reber in 198.

[13] Frank Coffield made this point about significance at the Ufi seminar on Surveying Motivation, Birmingham, December 2000. See 250; also 43, 44, 45.

[14] See 176, or any text on cost-benefit analysis.

[15] Such enforcement often happens in compulsory initial education.

Chapter 2:
Different faces of learning motivation

Four dimensions of motivation

Human motivation as felt energy for a goal forms as a person develops an intention to act. Specifically, it happens when the pros and cons of one goal are compared with one or more possible alternative goals. If the energy could be measured directly, like taking blood pressure, one might think there would only be a single value to be read off. But that is not so. Motivation is not single-valued; it is inherently multi-valued or fragmented, taking up different values even when directed towards the same action or decision. A person will normally only be aware of one of the values at once; but behind it lie other values, waiting in the wings to be summoned up almost at will. The values readily switch places, according to context. This is true for all motivation.

Multi-valued motivation to learn may be tricky to deal with, but it is not to be regretted. It is the result of processes which have evolved to be subtle and malleable, and which have endless potential to reflect the complexity of life. For policy-makers or researchers, the implication is that they must make sure that they get the right motivational value to study; or, at the very least, that they can tell them apart.

There are, in fact, four ways in which the different values can be categorized: by level of goal; by saliency of perception; by stage of action; and by the nature and degree of mental processing. We shall use these four dimensions in turn to pin down the shifting values of motivation for examination.

Goal level

In Chapter 1 we defined motivation in terms of keenness linked to action. Following many analysts we take the view that most people seek to organise their actions according to some kind of goal hierarchy, deliberately or otherwise.[1]

Figure 2.1 illustrates this with the example of somebody who is an ambitious teacher and a conscientious parent. He is committed to clear goals, and has established some order in his life. This exemplary person has, as top priority, general life-goals which are stable for long of periods of time, and which set a context for his daily action and moral behaviour. Life goals require intermediate goals or strategies to carry them out. These strategies provide the meaningful framework for his decisions about his actions: what they will involve, and how he will carry them out. Actions which express such strategies are, in effect, projects to achieve his life goals. Not all his actions are projects, thankfully. He can also act spontaneously, and on a whim. An intermediate goal or a project may do double duty, serving more than one life goal at once.

For clarity, Figure 2.1 shows only a small part of this person's goal hierarchy. In real life, individuals may have a number of life goals, declared or otherwise; and their projects are broken down further into routine actions (called 'scripts'). In our example, "Give pupils real responsibility for the school" might be expressed through a whole set of scripts: running a student council in the school; electing representatives from each class; and itself electing a representative for the area youth council.

This whole system is organised to implement individuals' life-goals in ways which they find most rewarding in overall terms. Strategy deals with long term, high level goals and their supporting intermediate goals; shorter term projects deal with tactics at a lower level to implement the strategy. High and low do not express an imposed value judgement here, but simply indicate a systematic priority relationship.

Goals and motivational balance
As projects develop, or as unexpected crises occur, personal experience gained from implementing strategy is fed back into the motivation system. If this does not produce the high-level payoff expected, either the strategy and its projects are adjusted until they do; or the high level goal may be changed to accommodate the experience; or a bit of both. Our conscientious teacher, for example, finds that even getting up at 5.45a.m. on weekdays does not enable him to keep on top of the paperwork. So he decides to get up early at weekends as well, in order to keep the daytime free for family activities. There may well come a time when even this is not enough to keep on top of the avalanche of official paperwork, and he will be faced with harder decisions about what makes an inspirational head teacher, and how to combine it with being a good parent. This reflects learning from experience.

Particular projects may have implications for a number of different higher level goals; an action which serves one goal may prove to be detrimental to another for example.[2] Project level actions commonly offer a balance of payoffs – some good, some bad – reflecting fundamental trade-offs or inconsistencies across the whole gamut of goals. It is this balance which stands at the centre

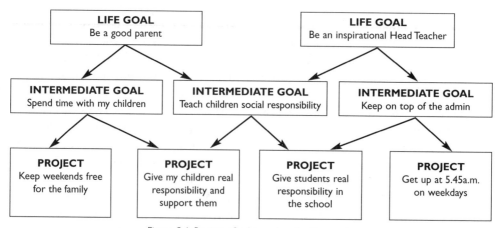

Figure 2.1 Portion of a hierarchy of action goals

of the motivational process for each action. Even if a planned action goes well in itself, the motivational balance may shift, because a separate disappointment elsewhere may cause a shift in high and/or intermediate goals. This then disturbs the balance of pay-offs for that particular action.

Such shifts are happening all the time, mainly at intermediate strategy level, but occasionally higher still. External conditions – in the family group, for example, or in the wider world – are always changing. Hierarchies can settle down into fixed patterns, but are commonly in various degrees of flux. Maintaining motivational balance in these conditions is what "keeping all the plates spinning" really means.

How far people succeed in maintaining their system of goals differs from person to person. Many people – either by force of circumstance or by choice – spend large amounts of time on auto-pilot, tolerating heavy inconsistency in their actions and goals in an attempt to maintain a settled pattern to daily living.[3] Some simply take each day as it comes, persistently ignoring information which indicates the need for them to re-appraise their various goals. This may work for a limited period, as a coping device, but the psychological pressure can undermine health and happiness, and cause serious strain in personal relationships.

Identifying the level

The intention which is the focus of any motivational assessment might be at any level in the goal hierarchy. The first rule of motivation enquiry is to pinpoint exactly which it is. For example, a survey question such as "How much does the idea of being fit and healthy in old age motivate you to take regular exercise?" is general.

It concerns a possible high level life goal, or an intermediate level goal which the respondent might see as a route to one or more high level goals. A survey question such as "How motivated are you to go jogging before breakfast?" is quite different, however. It is likely to be seen as specific, relating to tactics at a lower level in the goal hierarchy.

Surveys attempting this degree of precision must however be careful about interpreting responses. Identifying the action is not enough, for the same action can function at one level in one person's goal hierarchy and at another level in somebody else's hierarchy. The hierarchical level needs to be pinpointed in each case. Surveys which ask about motivation but which are not clear about goal level have very limited usefulness.

Saliency of the self

Saliency of the self is another key idea in understanding motivation. According to Deci & Ryan's widely-supported theory, any well-adjusted individual's identity is formed of multiple selves.[4]

At the centre of Figure 2.2 is the true self (the real me). Attached to this are a unique selection and pattern of specialised selves, corresponding to the significant roles which individuals develop as they come to maturity. These selves can readily be brought to the fore of awareness and attention, according to circumstances or the person's will, and – equally readily – they can be pushed into the psychological background. When any particular self is in the foreground it is said to be salient (literally, prominent).

Saliency is crucial to motivation because, at any one moment, whichever self is salient is

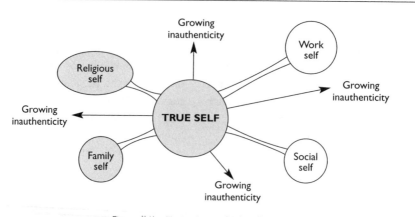

Figure 2.2   Illustrative multiple selves

the one which makes the motivational assessment and controls the motivational energy.[5] When saliency changes from one self to another, motivation will switch accordingly. In individuals whose identities are well integrated, the effect can be dramatic but benign – not unbalanced or sinister, as in the case of Dr Jekyll and Mr Hyde. As Figure 2.2 shows, when individuals have their true self salient, and act according to its goals, they will feel a strong sense of authenticity.[6] They will have a sense of being directly in touch with their basic needs and, in particular, will feel the satisfactions of autonomy strongly when the true self is in charge.

But every adult has to juggle other, less authentic selves as a routine part of daily life in pursuit of life goals: me the loyal worker; me the fitness fanatic; me the wine buff etc. These will each have their own, role-dependent, motivations. The demands of daily living mean that individuals tend to have a lead-self or role as a general default setting – me the business executive; me the parent, etc. – but switch saliency between selves according to internal or external prompting. When this happens, motivation associated with the non-salient selves will also drop into the background for the time

being, allowing mental and physical energy to be focused on achieving the goals of the self which has become salient.

When life is really complicated, we may feel literally torn by motivational indecision – making first one self salient, then another, and trying to reconcile different goals at the high level of general life strategy. If the goals are not reconcilable, we are faced with the choice of either (a) remaining in a state of virtual paralysis – pulled mentally first one way and then another, with no energy left for anything else – relying either on somebody else's decision or on accident to push us one way or another; or (b) plumping for one particular self and its goals, and leaving the other(s) to fade into the background. This 'plumping' is usually felt as a liberating experience, the relief seeming to offer further confirmation of the intended action goal. The so-called "mid-life crisis" is such a point, when adults may make a fundamental choice in favour of one or a selection of alternative selves, and reject the rest, with serious implications for their former range of roles and commitments.

Any particular self may be salient for very long periods.

Lisa is a lone parent and unemployed. Her social life is limited by a shortage of money, and she spends weeks on end with her 'Mum self' continuously salient. This is occasionally alleviated by the need to bring her 'occupational self' to the fore at the Jobcentre. She has little opportunity to air her fit and healthy 'lifestyle self', except when it is bruised on occasional visits to the doctor's surgery.

But sometimes saliency can switch in highly sensitive ways.[7]

Matt plays football regularly. One of his selves is 'me the loyal team member', and another is 'me the star performer'. When he's playing football, Matt switches saliency repeatedly between these two. If a goal is scored, 'Matt the team player' comes to the fore: we scored it; similarly, if the game is lost, we lost it and we feel badly about it. On the other hand, Matt might flip to the star performer's viewpoint more or less at any time, thinking: I scored the winning goal, or I let myself down.

Players like Matt (and, indeed, the fans that identify with them) typically flip from one salient self to another many times in a match. Sports coaches normally try hard to keep the we-dimension salient for as much of the game as possible, but unfortunately there is no sure-fire way to control saliency switches. A young player might flip from team player to competitive individual merely at the sight of a parent or friend or team scout on the touch-line.

If you want to ask people like Lisa or Matt about their motivation, you will need to establish which self is responding to the question, and how authentic they feel that self to be.

Stages in the action cycle

Once people have made up their mind on a project goal, according to the salient self, their motivation system makes variable degrees of energy available to pursue it. Figure 2.3 shows how this part of the motivation process unfolds in a cycle.[8] This cycle is about action, and should not be confused with David Kolb's experiential learning circle, which is about how new knowledge sinks into the brain.

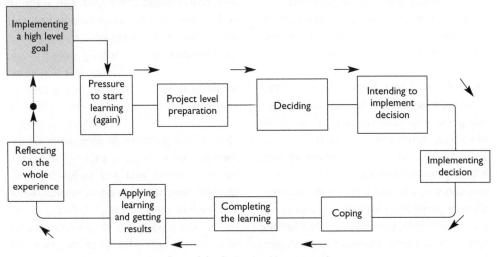

Figure 2.3   Project-level learning cycle

The cycle operates according to the needs of higher level goals. Individuals work their way through it as they move from thinking about a possibility; to deciding on an action; to planning and implementing the decision; to taking action; to coping with difficulties if they arise; to completing and getting the fruits of completion; and finally to thinking about all that experience.[9] Then, if the higher level goals are unchanged, another cycle can begin on another learning project. Otherwise, things go on hold until the higher level strategic direction is sorted out.

The action cycle applies to learning as well as to other things. Sometimes learners will move through the cycle rapidly, and sometimes not. They may be able to take various stages as read, according to prior experience. In the sphere of learning the action cycle shows up clearly in formal courses of learning which are designed to shadow it. But it is also found in the more spontaneous forms of informal intentional learning. Everyone has a number of such action cycles on the go at any one time. In real life, of course, learning cycles are seldom quite as neat and tidy as Figure 2.3 implies. It is common for people to have to retrace some of their steps, and go through some of the stages more than once in a cycle.

The key point here is that the motivation individuals feel for the learning depends on the point they have reached in the cycle. Motivation is not solely about the decision stage. The motivational assessment process is kept going throughout the cycle, more or less continuously and with varying degrees of effort; and the motivational energy for the learning changes accordingly. It is like the athlete, constantly reappraising her performance as she goes round the track, her

motivation rising or falling according to how she is doing. The basic fact is that motivation alters around the cycle, and it can only be properly understood when its position in the cycle is pinned down.

Motivational changes in the cycle
Some of the motivational changes during the cycle may be due to saliency switching. Others may be due to the input of new information. This might be about external factors, or the individual's progress and performance relative to other people's, or about changes elsewhere in the goal hierarchy which may affect the value of the learning.

These rather straightforward sources of change are not the only ones at work, however. Some of the changes are inherent in the cycle itself, reflecting changes of mind-set.[10] An individual's motivational assessment depends on the mind-set at the time the assessment is made: different mind-set, different assessment. Sometimes one thing will be accentuated, and sometimes another, and the field of view and sharpness of focus will vary too. Changes in mind-set are rather like phase-changes of the kind seen in nature when water becomes ice, or tadpole becomes frog. Something fundamental seems to happen to motivation at two specific points in the learning cycle – once, when initial interest becomes decision; and again, when decision becomes implementation.

One of the great accomplishments of the evolved human brain is that it can readily switch between real and virtual modes.[11] Humans have the ability to use experience and imagination in virtual fashion, to rehearse and predict the likely consequences of action mentally, without stirring from the armchair. In the initial-interest mind-set, the potential learner is constructing a kind of virtual motivation. This can be virtually experienced, talked about and investigated, using a kind of virtual intention.

At some point, on or soon after the person makes a decision, a real intention is formed, replacing the virtual one. This is when the decisional mind-set takes hold. It is this sense of real commitment which marks the phase change. Appraisal is now at its broadest, and the motivation now feels different because it is real. The mind reacts differently to experiences which are real, compared with those which are dreamlike, or where reality is knowingly suspended.

Later on, an implementation mind-set develops. Studies show that the mind in this state tends to pigeon-hole most doubts and difficulties, and focuses the individual's attention very strongly on what has to be done and the prizes to be won. Motivation is reworked accordingly in "Go for it!" mode. If failure threatens, the learner can break out of the implementation mind-set and backtrack to the decisional or initial-interest mind-sets.

Surveying motivation
According to this analysis, social scientists who focus on what people are interested in, and the intensity of the interest, are probably working in the area of virtual motivation. Those who study the real choices people make are more likely to be in the area of real intentions and the decisional mind-set. But if they are examining learners who have started and who are not failing, they may well be tapping into the implementation mind-set.

If a survey is to produce accurate information about motivation for learning, it has to discover: first what action cycle each respondent is concerned with; second where the respondent is in that cycle; and third what mind-set he or she has in place.

Degrees of mental processing
The last aspect of motivation explored here concerns the mental activity or effort which a person puts into the appraisal that produces motivation. Mental processing covers all this.

Broadly speaking, there are three kinds of mental processing: the rational, conscious kind; the routine auto-pilot kind; and fully fledged, uncontrolled subconscious activity.

Rational mental processing is essentially verbal, where a dialogue inside the head deals in facts, opinions, expectations, etc.[12] The person is conscious of mental activity, and can in principle talk about it in some sort of language. The degree of attention individuals pay to this internal dialogue is likely to vary, from person to person, and from time to time for the same person. It has long been a feature of some cultures to assume that rational thinking is intrinsically better than other kinds of thinking. No such value judgement is made here. People are generally sparing in their use of rational appraisal, for the same reason that some people are reluctant to begin moving plants in a garden: one thing leads to another, and then to another, and very soon it looks too much like hard work. In the multi-layered world of action goals, it can all get complicated pretty quickly. Decisions tend to be made on the basis of relatively little information, even with the extraordinary power of the human brain available. People generally use routines, stereotypes and social norms to short-circuit a lot of thinking. They also tolerate high levels of inaccuracy relating to the goals we adopt, and are correspondingly slow to rethink their actions and to refresh their motivations.

Routine mental processing, as if on autopilot, is exemplified by car-driving, or the level of mental activity that copes with any routine chore. Here an action has become so habituated that it can be carried out almost automatically, below immediate awareness and with the minimum of conscious thought. But it is not actually unconscious; it is an extreme version of rational processing, where the main focus of the person's attention is currently engaged elsewhere. In such cases there is a degree of conscious control and, by switching focus, the person can instantly restore the processing into a fully rational, verbal state.[13] The overwrought mother, desperately trying to prepare a family meal and speak to a colleague on the telephone at the same time, is likely to drop both if she hears a shriek of fear or pain from the next room. She has been monitoring the infant all along. Even in the routine part of the process, motivation is a product of rationality. Having a large part of the hierarchy of action goals running on auto-pilot might seem as if no conscious processing means no motivation. But routine activity is a process so familiar, that people simply do not need to attend to the motivation for it for much of the time, freeing attention for less routine events, or for the pleasure of daydreaming. Focus on motivation can, however, be reasserted at will.

Subconscious mental processing is essentially uncontrollable. Most psychologists believe such processing goes on ceaselessly and can only be glimpsed by

implication, or possibly through fantasy and dreams. This is a mental world where the salient self (itself a fabrication of the rational mind) cannot go, and which it could not verbalise about, even if it did.[14] The subconscious and the conscious mind interact closely. The subconscious appears to make judgements – often almost instantaneously – which influence the person's emotions and behaviour. It will often steal a march on the comparatively lumbering rational process; or contribute to states of internal conflict, where the rational mind offers one solution and the subconscious urges something utterly different (through the gut feeling). If this conflict results in feelings of unease and personal inauthenticity, the salient self can use these in the rational process as evidence in assessing situations and choices.

Mental processing is influenced by these three types of mental activity systems. But there are additional factors also at work. Much depends on the effort the person puts into the processing, and the skills and habits of assessment deployed. Some individuals can discover more motivation in an action than others would do, because they have more skills to think the implications through and to assemble relevant information; or because they may avoid habitual biases or reactions which limit the motivational outcome. Mood can also play a part. Studies of mood, for example, show that the happier people are, the less mental processing they are inclined to do; and depressed people tend to look harder for good news, or fall into seemingly endless ruminations to put off the pain of decision.[15]

Motivation and brain systems

What we have described in this chapter so far is a process of internal appraisal where individuals, adopting a salient self, review the perceived implications of an intentional goal or action, and feel degrees of keenness for the goal or action as a result. This motivation can be at project or strategic level, and it can be virtual or real, according to the stage in the action cycle. People are aware of the motivations they have; they can talk about them, and can recapture the main features of the appraisal itself.

This seems to imply that motivational states reflect rational processing alone. But rationality is by no means the whole picture. Here we look a little more closely at the way the various elements work together.

The brain seems, in effect, to operate two largely separate, but interpenetrating, brain systems simultaneously.[16] There is a non-verbal, high-primate system, operating below the threshold of rational awareness. In evolutionary terms, this represents the original, instinctive and intuitive brain functions of proto-humans, before the great leap into language and symbolic thought was made. It has been overlaid but never replaced. On top of this – and not always synchronised with it – operates the rational, verbal brain system of modern human beings.

The older system is hard to know, but experimental psychologists generally agree it is rapid, snap-judgmental and instinctive. It operates holistically, taking an overview of a complex environmental opportunity or threat, rather than analysing its separate attributes. It is non-verbal, and draws very largely on memory banks of past experiences, where past situations are coded with basic nasty/nice labels for instant recognition by the emotions. As new situations arise, they are matched back to the memory

bank. A nasty match triggers avoidance action, a nice match prepares for approach.

This brain system, it seems, has little or no capacity to rehearse mentally, or to create expectations – let alone theories. It deals with if/then causal relationships as subconsciously remembered correlation: "If I put my hand in a flame, my hand will hurt and be sore for a long time". It has little need for elaboration of identity, beyond the most primitive 'me' of the responding animal. But, for all these limitations, it is speedy and complex in its workings. It is good at recognising faces and reading stress responses on them, and very good at sniffing out potential threats.[17]

By contrast, the rational brain system is essentially verbal, and its currency is narrative. Its memory banks store verbal facts, coded for emotional implications. But there are also banks of conceptual knowledge including self-knowledge, behavioural norms, imaginings, and much else – all of it verbal, and all material which can in principle be raised to awareness.[18] Its processes are slow by comparison with the non-verbal brain system. They are, however, deliberative, analytical, and propositional, and offer the capacity to create whole private worlds of imagination and foresight, which stretch understanding far beyond what is learned through experience. It enables us to appreciate and produce beauty; but it also provides us with the capability to develop sophisticated, life-destroying inventions.

It is no accident that adults and older children cannot remember the period of their lives which pre-dates speech. The arrival of speech is the developmental point when the rational brain system is 'booted-up', like a computer. Before that, the non-verbal system has sole charge. Happily it has evolved the potential to clear the way for full awareness and its rational functions to come on stream.

All this strongly suggests that each person has two motivational faculties: one within the realm of awareness and language; and another lurking in the shadows beyond awareness, and operating instinctively. We saw earlier how emotions triggered by the second can become evidence for the first.[19]

Deep in the non-verbal system are the natural needs and instincts which all people are born with, but which may vary somewhat in relative intensity between individuals. These include life-based needs for nourishment, sex, protection, etc., and the general seeking of pleasure and the avoidance of pain which helps to achieve them. Three such needs which are particularly relevant to learning, and which interlock and support each other, are competence, affiliation, and autonomy.[20]

- **Competence** is really a thirst to find out how the world works.[21] We see this in the infant-as-scientist, with a powerful curiosity to identify and to solve the "what...if" puzzles that lead to understanding of the world: "What happens if I put my fingers in here/throw this thing there/mix these together?"

- **Affiliation** is the need to love and be loved.[22] This is essential for the long gestation and developmental periods that successful human reproduction needs, and to the effective group living that supports them.

- **Autonomy** is the need to be a proactive agent.[23] This is the instinct which leads people to try things out for themselves, and to be prepared to challenge authority

in doing so. It promotes action and, by extension, the leadership needed for strong community life. It abhors passivity.

Well designed learning experiences target these fundamental needs. Experiments show that this improves motivation, without people really knowing quite how the trick is done. It is likely that in such cases the non-verbal brain is registering a feel-good factor, and labelling the experience in the subconscious memory as, "Rewarding: let's have more of it". When these needs are not addressed, "It's boring!" or "It's bad! Avoid it!"

What seems to be happening in these cases is that there are indeed two motivation processes running in parallel. The one that we are aware of belongs to the rational brain system; the non-verbal process stimulates or inhibits us without our knowing how or why; we feel strangely encouraged, or strangely discouraged, over and above the motivation we know about, depending on how well served our instinctive basic needs are behind the mental curtain. These buzz-factors can amplify the rational motivation process, on the basis that our gut-feeling can be taken as confirming or disconfirming the rationally based motivation. The emotions work, in effect, like rockets attached to a space probe: they can both boost motivation and put a brake on it.

The interdependence of rationality and emotionality adds essential human warmth to what would otherwise be a cold and calculating process. People who are sensitive to these effects can enjoy a far richer experience than those who fend them off. If the emotional and rational motivation systems both point towards a particular intention, extraordinary motivational energy can result. If they are in conflict, then the learner's motivation will be ambivalent and vulnerable.

This inter-penetration is very useful in evolutionary terms. It prevents people becoming the kind of exclusively rational calculators who may threaten life itself. It marries high-level mental capacity with instinctive roots. On the other hand, acting on the basis of gut-feeling alone produces results which are too unpredictable for rational appraisal. It is too erratic, unsystematic and too short-sighted, in fact, to play a predominant role in motivation. It may buy short-term excitement, and even win you a fat sum at the races, but it is not a sound basis for motivation in the longer term. Humans need body, soul and mind working together.

So, to understand a person's motivation, it is not enough to look at where it is in the action hierarchy; and at its saliency; and at the learning stage the person has reached. We must also ask about the amount of mental processing which goes into the motivation; and how far that is rooted in, and sensitive to, the inscrutable mental world of the subconscious.

Notes and references (Numbers refer to publications listed in the Reference section)

[1] See 38.
[2] The goal hierarchy serves as a map where the costs and benefits of an action can be found. This is fundamental in motivation.
[3] Eraut discusses this auto pilot in 79.
[4] See 202 for a useful account of the Deci & Ryan position; also 60.
[5] See 141, 144 & 155 for discussion of saliency and the self.
[6] This stress on authenticity is due to Deci & Ryan. See 202; also 216 & 217.
[7] Zander explores such switches in teams in 249.
[8] See 68 for a recent motivational analysis broadly along the same lines as here.
[9] See 51 for the approach to decision; also 88. For action and implementation, see 105 & 107. For a general account of coping see 162.
[10] See Gollwitzer 104, 106 & 107.
[11] This real/virtual distinction is the authors' clarification.
[12] See 144.
[13] See Eraut 79.
[14] See 77; also 146 & 159.
[15] See 92.
[16] See 77, 146 & 159.
[17] See 55; also 14.
[18] See Hoyle et al 144.
[19] See 92.
[20] These needs are the subject of renewed attention. See generally 128; also Deci & Ryan 202, 203 & 204.
[21] See Skinner 212 & 213; also 57; and Gropnik et al for the 'scientist in the crib' 112.
[22] See Leary & Baumeister 163.
[23] See 47, 54, 61, 62, 180, 188 & 203.

Chapter 3:
Motivation for learning activity

Introduction

So far we have seen that motivation:

- has a multiplicity of values, in terms of goal level, saliency, action stage, and mental processing;
- is produced by an internal assessment process, taking place in the brain's verbal system, but drawing some emotional evidence from more instinctive brain functions.

We now look in more detail at the basic framework for the internal assessment. This chapter explores the project level, and the next chapter will examine the strategic level.

At project level, this framework is common to all mature people, although the settings of the framework and the information flow running through the process are unique to each individual. These settings and flows vary according to many factors: genetic inheritance, experience, goal-level, action stage and mind-set, saliency, assessment skills, and cultural environment. They control the inputs, rigour, and style that we each apply to the components of our motivation.

It is precisely because the settings and information flows are open to a large degree of influence that motivation can be increased or reduced. Sometimes we are aware of the influence, and may even impose it on ourselves; sometimes it works subtly through our experience and environment. An under-standing of the basic framework and its information flows is needed before we can see where the triggers are which can change the motivational result.

First we look closely at the elements in basic motivation assessment, and how they work together. We shall use well-established theory to highlight the role of the various elements; to explain how motivation is created; and how – through the various settings and information flows – it can vary so dramatically from person to person, and from time to time. Then we shall look at a number of significant aspects of assessment itself. The example of Marie will help to illustrate various points.[1]

Marie is a 39-year-old single parent of 17-year-old twins, Zoe and Zak. She gave up work as a qualified nurse when her children were born and, following divorce five years later, subsequently patchworked together a variety of part-time jobs. She also does voluntary work at a local hospice, which she loves, and she makes twice-weekly visits to her frail mother who lives in a nursing home 25 miles away. Prompted by her friend, Bella, Marie has recently begun to think about returning to nursing as a full-time career. Zoe and Zak are due to spend a couple of months in the USA with their father before starting university, and they would like to keep in touch with Marie by e-mail. Marie's total lack of computer skills has suddenly become an issue, in terms both of career development and of family contact. An IT course at the local Further Education College has caught her eye.

Elements of motivational assessment at project level

Figure 3.1 summarises the main elements in the assessment process which creates project-level motivation to learn. These elements apply specifically to learning, but they also apply generally, and incorporate basic theory about how motivation works in more or less any field.

The basic theory

The basic theory, captured in the white boxes in Figure 3.1, is centred on probabilities and values as assessed by the individual, regarding a possible activity.[2] The boxes show that there are two inputs: the total anticipated net value, and the probability of

getting the net value (of the learning, in this case), both taken as perceived by the individual. Net value is the value to the learner after the perceived costs and benefits are taken into account. Probability of getting the net value summarises a whole gamut of the person's probability judgements about the learning activity, and the chances of it being successful.[3] Considering these two inputs, each of which reflects a number of more detailed considerations, produces motivation.

Just how motivation is created in this way is very important to our whole enquiry. If the relationship between inputs and the motivational output is seen as an equation, the question is what functional form that equation has. There are certain clues to this, which derive from logic and experience.

One property we would want it to have is that, if either of the two factors is zero,

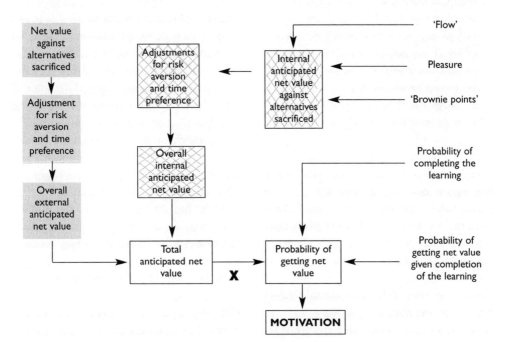

Figure 3.1 Motivation for a project level goal

motivation itself is zero. If individuals perceive absolutely no net value from learning, they will not have any motivation to do it. Even when they concede that there is net value, if they think there is no chance at all of their getting it, they will not have any motivation either.

We would also want to say that motivation should increase, if either net value or probability of realising it were to increase on its own. Lower probability turns people off, and so also does lower net value. Correspondingly, higher probability and higher net value each enhance motivation, when taken on their own.

When Marie is at the point of deciding to sign up for the computer course, her motivation wavers. She thinks her chances of succeeding are not good. Her friend Bella invites her round to have an evening on her computer, and Marie finds it less complicated than she thought. She now thinks that the chances of success are brighter, and signs up for the course in a fresh surge of keenness. Shortly afterwards, staffing at the hospice is restructured, and new posts are advertised. She has the necessary nursing experience, but the adverts ask for "evidence of IT competence". This makes her all the more determined to do the course.

Assuming (as initially we do) that probability is independent of value, and vice versa, altering the one will not alter the other.[4] It would follow that motivation would rise if both the assessed net value and probability increase; and, correspondingly, that motivation will fall if both factors fall.

These properties of the motivational process mean that motivation is, at very least, an increasing function of net value and probability. But a robust theory needs more. There

are all sorts of increasing equations that would have these properties. There are cases where large increases in inputs would produce tiny increases in motivation; or where the more the inputs increase, the less motivation grows; or where increases in the inputs leads to ever greater motivation, in a sort of log-rolling effect.

The research of psychologists over many years points strongly, although not invariably, towards the last of these.[5] Marie knows what this means.

Marie got keener and keener about her IT course. The more certain she became that she could complete the course satisfactorily, and the more value she saw in the work, the more her enthusiasm seemed to run ahead of her. She had a breakthrough. What had been mountains became molehills; and suddenly the sky was the limit.

This sort of relationship between inputs and outputs represents economies of scale. In mathematical terms, the relationship is multiplicative: motivation is related to the multiplication of probability and net value. If the relationship is multiplicative, growing each input factor equally by a given proportion would mean that motivation itself would grow by even more. Moreover, if just one of the two factors grows, the larger the other factor is, the more it adds to motivation. It has, in fact, been a standard contention in psychology for half a century that motivation is linked to the two inputs in just such a way.[6] This would be true not just in the learning sphere, but generally.

This proposition is the basis of the classic so-called valency/expectancy model of motivation formulated by psychologists. For the

Key

M   = motivation   P   = perceived probability of realising value
V   = net perceived value   f   = a function of

If we could measure motivation, net value and probability on continuous numerical scales, we would, in principle, be able to sum up the theory in the general expression:

$$M = f (V \times P)$$

V and P correspond to the two white input boxes in Fig. 3.1. The function f would have the characteristics that if either V or P is zero, motivation is zero; and that the partial derivatives of M with respect to V and P are both positive and functions of the level of the other variable, and that the second order partial derivatives are also positive.

Figure 3.2   General valency / expectancy model

benefit of those with a mathematical bent, Figure 3.2 shows this model expressed as a general formula – it can be skipped without loss.

According to this theory, then, motivation is a kind of feeding frenzy. The faster net value and probability are thrown into the process, the faster the motivational appetite grows. This seems quite plausible, at a common-sense level.

If Bill tries to encourage the reluctant Ben with some low level incentives, Ben's motivation is hard to shift. But as Bill raises incentives higher and higher, there comes a point where Ben's motivation does start to increase, and after that Bill feels it's more and more like pushing at an open door.

Testing this theory has been complicated, not least by the lack of available measures of the two inputs, expressed as continuous numerical scales. For the most part there are just the banded measures examined in Chapter 1. Expressed in these terms, the

multiplicative assumption has to be shown rather imprecisely, as in Figure 3.3. Here, banded measures of positive and negative net value are along the vertical axis, and bands of probability are on the horizontal axis. These inputs are then merged to produce a final banding for overall motivation.

In the multiplicative theory, when either value or probability is zero, motivation is also zeroed out (any sum multiplied by zero makes zero). That accounts for the zero column and row in the table. As for the rest, if the probability band is held constant, motivational ratings in the illustration consistently show that an increase in value produces a positive – or at any rate a non-negative – effect on motivation: and the same is true the other way round. What is more, they show a rather broad-brush amplification of motivation if both factors are positive, and both are raised to higher levels.

Validating the theory in this form would mean, at the very least, taking banded measures of perceived net value and probability

Probability

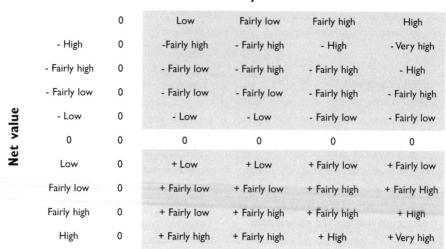

Net value	0	Low	Fairly low	Fairly high	High
- High	0	-Fairly high	- Fairly high	- High	- Very high
- Fairly high	0	- Fairly low	- Fairly high	- Fairly high	- High
- Fairly low	0	- Fairly low	- Fairly low	- Fairly high	- Fairly high
- Low	0	- Low	- Low	- Fairly low	- Fairly low
0	0	0	0	0	0
Low	0	+ Low	+ Low	+ Fairly low	+ Fairly low
Fairly low	0	+ Fairly low	+ Fairly low	+ Fairly high	+ Fairly High
Fairly high	0	+ Fairly low	+ Fairly high	+ Fairly high	+ High
High	0	+ Fairly high	+ Fairly high	+ High	+ Very high

Figure 3.3   Motivation function tabulated in bands

across a range of input conditions, and seeing if an individual's banded motivational responses approach the pattern shown in the table.

Much more research is needed into these issues of functional form. Tests done over the years suggest that the process is likely to be multiplicative, but they allow the possibility that it may not be. Two things are particularly worth noting, in the learning context:

• There is some evidence that where the value is heavily influenced by pleasing other people (e.g. parents or employers), or where the action is undertaken as a matter of principle, the amplifying effect may not appear.[7] Motivation would still increase a bit, as value or probability are seen to grow; but there would not be a speeding up effect at higher values of these factors.

• There may be complications if judgements of value and of subjective probability are not – as assumed above – independent of each other. This often happens in educational contexts, for example, if a learning goal is so difficult that only especially gifted or very hardworking people can hope to succeed. The kudos of succeeding at very difficult tasks has a correspondingly high perceived value, so the lower the probability (i.e. the higher the difficulty) the higher the value; and vice versa. This seesaw effect is why it is widely thought that goals of intermediate difficulty may be the most motivating for the average learner.[8] Harder goals would gain value, but lose probability even faster; easier goals have lower value, but gain in probability. Somewhere in the middle ground is a high point of motivation, where the seesaw between value and probability is best poised.

• These complications would appear to arise only in special circumstances; they do not really undermine the multiplicative formula as such, but rather make it more difficult to stoke up both probability and value together, so as to reach the point where motivation begins to run away with itself.

The conclusion to draw from all this is clear. The precise shape of the functional form that combines net value and probability to produce motivation needs to be determined in context, for each person and for each group. Whether it is multiplicative should be decided by the evidence.

What contributes to net value and probability?

We now return to Figure 3.1, to see how the two composite factors – overall net value and the probability of getting the value – are themselves made up. In each case there are a number of building-blocks. These provide a check list for policy-makers, for this is where leverage can be applied which will shift motivation in any desired direction.

How likely am I to get the net value?
Figure 3.1 shows how the learner's view of the probability of getting the net value is made up of the subjective probability of successfully completing the learning and the subjective probability of getting the net value, given completion of learning. If these components are independent of each other, the overall probability of getting the value is the product of the two. However likely I am to jump through one hoop, for example, my chances of jumping through two in succession are much less. If each hoop represents a one-in-ten chance, the chance that I shall jump clear through two in succession is one-in-a-hundred.

Marie had to think hard about doing her IT course. Could she be computer literate and

succeed in getting a new nursing job at the hospice? There seemed a reasonable chance she would finish the course, and get the qualification. But then she still had to land a post at the hospice, or go out and find another job that fitted in with all the other things she had to do. Given the competition from younger people, who had grown up with computers, she was less confident about that. Putting the two things together suddenly made the whole undertaking seem more problematic.

Probability of successfully completing the learning
Two major factors help people to estimate their chances here:
• their belief that they have both the ability and the resources to complete the specific learning to the necessary standard. Psychologists call this self-efficacy (and there is no practicable alternative to the professional jargon here); [9]
• their belief that fate will not intervene to blow the learning off course, commonly known as bad luck.[10] It marks the vulnerability that people feel in trying to carry through the learning in practical terms. Those who are poor or sick, for example, or whose home lives are exceptionally complicated, may well be fatalistic about their chances, irrespective of the effort or ability they apply.

Self-efficacy and bad luck are probably not independent of each other, and are likely to be tied in a multiplicative relationship, amplifying each other.

Self-efficacy – numerous studies have found self-efficacy to be a key ingredient in motivation.[11] It has significant power to explain people's attitudes and behaviour in a wide range of domains, including health, phobias, athletics, and learning. It has a general form, where individuals have a broad but unspecified confidence in achievement, such as, "I am a very capable sort of person". But it also has a specific form, where the confidence relates to a particular sphere, like learning, and to the particular goal under consideration. It is the specific form which really counts in explaining motivation in particular circumstances.

These specific self-efficacy beliefs are very closely bound up with experience. If, for example, individuals experience a learning failure, their self-efficacy takes a knock — and, in some conditions, a complete nose dive. If new learning is proposed, their damaged self-efficacy makes it more difficult to raise motivation again. As success depends on strong motivation, any attempt at repeat learning in this state is likely to fail again, producing even more damage to self-efficacy — "See? I knew I couldn't do it". So, over time, self-efficacy can be driven down in a vicious circle.[12]

But the reverse can also apply. Success bolsters self efficacy, so that motivation for repeat learning grows. Up to certain broad limits, this leads to a virtuous circle of more success, and greater and greater increases in self-efficacy. How a person's self-efficacy is ratcheted up or down over a succession of learning experiences largely depends on the standard of achievement assumed for each learning task. The individual can set this personally, but often it will be externally imposed, through qualifications for example, or be set by family expectations or social norms. If the standard is set very high, self-efficacy can collapse, even before learning begins. The best way to build up specific self-efficacy over time is to set challenging, but not over-testing, standards.[13] Setting very

easy targets is not an answer, because people need to make some degree of effort if they are to value the progress they make.

In the learning sphere, specific self-efficacy is itself a combination of beliefs about two things: the idea of inborn ability, often seen narrowly as IQ; and the perceived ability to work hard at the given task.[14] When people are in the coping stage of a learning project, the causes to which they attribute emerging failure will often centre on these two matters.[15] Work-levels are generally something which can be improved, but the thought that "I am just not bright enough" is inescapable. This is not something external, where the responsibility for failure can be shuffled off. It is internal and too close to home.

Teachers often exhort failing children to work harder, because the implications of telling them they are not able enough would be devastating. Children become almost obsessed with mutual comparisons. They are not slow to spot such teacherly evasion. What is more, many children will talk themselves into beliefs about their own lack of ability which are simply false, with very damaging motivational consequences.

Parents also have difficulty over their children's self-efficacy.[16] Many are preoccupied with how bright their children are, and commonly believe that children have natural inborn limitations to their learning performance. This is a kind of entity belief that there is some real thing in the brain, which limits performance — rather in the way that the size of a car's engine limits its maximum acceleration. Parents naturally want to feel that their children have enough of what it takes to secure a comfortable life on their own account. They often unwittingly praise brightness to the point where their children are driven constantly to compare themselves with others in the IQ stakes. In these conditions, the slightest failure at school can open up a chasm of self-doubt in a child, reflected in low self-efficacy for learning, which may last a lifetime.

On the other hand, if parents stress the importance of effort and concentration more than native talent, children may be encouraged to see failure as something they can change. Those who do will have a more robust response, higher self-efficacy, and consequently higher motivation.

Bad luck – Even if self-efficacy is high, individuals may still have little confidence that some spanner will not be put into the works by external forces beyond their control. In this case their assurance of success extends only so far as they believe that such impediments will not crop up. It is only too easy to become a habitual dropout from learning on this account. This is where access to good social/family support can make the difference between eventual success or repeated failure.

Against this background, each individual will assess the probability of successfully completing the learning by weighing up together the two components – self-efficacy, itself a matter of effort and ability, and bad luck.

Marie felt she could do her course well enough. She was a hard worker, and the tutor assured her that she would be able to understand the material. But something always seemed to crop up. Her mother needed frequent visits, to stop her sinking into depression, and the car was well past reliable. She was going to have to replace it sooner or

later. When Marie felt tired or low, she tended to be fatalistic about her chances. She had to balance the whole thing out. She supposed there was a fair chance she could 'hack it', as Zak put it, but it was very much a matter of keeping her fingers crossed.

Probability of getting the net value, given completion of learning
This probability depends on the make-up of the overall net value. If, for example, a major element of value is the prospect of getting a better paid job as a result of learning, there is always a chance that this may not happen, even if the learning itself is carried through. Similarly for other bits of value too. The broad judgement represented by this probability therefore depends on how far the various components of value are assured or not.

Marie is very keen on the idea of keeping in touch with the twins electronically – she is going to miss them dreadfully. But there is a chance that they will be too absorbed in their new lives to keep in touch regularly. And the hospice job was just too good to come true, too. So even if the course itself went well, she might be little better off in the end. On the other hand, Bella seemed convinced that if Marie completed the course, it would all pay off one way or another – perhaps in a way she could not see now. Marie came to think that, on balance, Bella was probably right.

The summary probability can be analysed into two elements, just as in the earlier case: first in terms of the individual's beliefs about personal efficacy (a) to extract the value which the completed learning makes possible, and (b) the external luck factor in doing so.

To sum up the whole probability side of the model (see the pale grey boxes in Figure 3.1), we can see how several of the individual's specific beliefs about probability are drawn together into an overall probability assessment. Sometimes these beliefs will be assessed carefully – even too carefully. But assessment at this project level will usually be cursory and vague, and be dominated by extrapolations from personal experience. It will also depend on the currently salient self, and the stage of learning – with its differing mind-sets – that the learner has reached.

Most of the key probability considerations are dealt with here. But the risk of any particular expected payoff proving disappointing, once it has been achieved – "The job didn't pay so well as I hoped"– is taken as a risk-discount on the value side of the model.

What is the net value of the learning?
We can now follow through on the net value components of the process shown in Figure 3.1. Total anticipated net value consists of external and internal elements (shown in dark grey and crosshatch, respectively). Each is assessed against an alternative which the person has sacrificed in choosing to do the learning.

External net value – This accrues to the individual. It is net value which the learner gets which is conditional on the external context. Something other than the learning has to happen to enable the learner to gain the value – the existence of a new and better job, for example; or improved social life from new contacts made through the learning; or some form of altruistic thrill from seeing a benefit which the learning gives to somebody else. This is extrinsic value, contributing extrinsic motivation.

In Marie's case, there is the prospect of a more regular income she would have from getting the hospice job. But, more immediately, there is also the pleasure she knows Zoe and Zak will get from seeing her overcome her fear of computers; and their reduced concern about her, as they leave home, if she can restore an up-to-date, developing career.

Internal net value – is net value which is an inherent feature of the learning process, and/or of its completion, or in some other sense that does not in any way rely on external factors. This is often called intrinsic net value, giving rise to intrinsic motivation.

Marie's intrinsic net value begins with her own sense of achievement. Then there is the sheer pleasure she gets from being a member of a learning group, the stimulating computer software she can use whenever she wants, and the fascination of learning in a completely new area. Sometimes she loses herself in the work, and her friends have to tell her it is time to go.

All manner of different net values can arise under the two headings external and internal. Figure 3.3 shows these brought together, and summed up as a judgement for each heading. The summing up will involve some implicit use of weighting for importance, and reflect the size or significance of the different net value elements. For example, in extrinsic motivation, gains in job satisfaction may be more important than a better pay scale. Or being top of the class may be more important than enjoying the learning. As the discussion of probability above noted, the depth of assessment can vary from the detailed and scrupulous to the skimpy and minimal, and will depend upon saliency and learning stage.

In the external category, assessment starts at the top with the basic judgmental process. This sets the net costs against the benefits that will accrue from the learning, as perceived by the learner. Several different types of value and cost may be involved in this, and their perceived relative size and importance will be influential in the merging process.

Further judgmental allowances then have to be made, one for risk and the other for time preference.

• Most people are averse to risk, and will reduce riskier net value – compared to more certain value – in making their judgements. This is why, for example, bankers are so concerned with confidence in financial markets; if risks suddenly grow – a new war in the Middle East, perhaps – perceived net values of financial assets fall, and motivation falls too.

Marie could not be sure just what salary might go with a nursing post at the hospice, so she decided to assume it would be on the low side initially. In any case she was sure that it was better to get into a regular pay structure, rather than rely on bits of part-time work. There were plans to extend the work of the hospice – it was unlikely to close, as the cottage hospital had done – and the job there was likely to be a permanent post. She highly valued the prospect of getting it.

• Similarly, most people fundamentally prefer to get their hands on potential value sooner, rather than later – this is called time-preference in investment behaviour. The net value has to be judgmentally adjusted up or down according to whether the payoff comes swiftly or

slowly. Psychological evidence points to very large inconsistencies, even irrationalities, in the behaviour of many people if they are asked to assess various combinations of delayed net value.[17]

After individuals have allowed in their judgement for the relative size and importance of different aspects of net value, and then after further allowances for risk and time preference, they reach their final view on overall net value against a sacrificed alternative. Figure 3.3 shows that – other things being equal – the higher this overall value is felt to be, the greater the motivation will be.

Internal value, on the right hand side of Figure 3.1, can be seen in a similar way. Adjusting for risk and time preference is very much the same as we have already seen. The only thing to add is that here the intrinsic values tend to be more tangible and more immediate than extrinsic values, so that the effect of the adjustment is less.

Three basic components make up intrinsic net value: flow, pleasure, and Brownie points.

• **Flow**, in its full form, is an exhilarating, almost dreamlike state of intense absorption in an activity, which arises from fulfilling basic instinctive needs.[18] This condition is sometimes experienced by athletes undertaking record-breaking feats; by mountaineers operating at full stretch to overcome a near impossible pitch; by scientists and inventors pushing their knowledge into new realms; by dancers and musicians totally lost in the performance of a difficult work. It is a high, almost transformed, state of consciousness, where actions seem to flow along. At lower levels the person's mind is strongly engaged and interested. At high levels people feel they transcend their normal physical limitations, and call flow a spiritual experience. Research in real life situations shows that individuals are most likely to experience flow when they manage to match a challenge with their own effort and skill.[19] The feeling has great value for people who experience it, and can be motivating to the point of being almost addictive. In learning it is most likely to happen in contexts which allow the learner to have autonomy.

• **Pleasure** is more sensual, associated with physical experience. It works through consumer satisfaction to create consumption benefits. In learning, pleasure may be prompted by the qualities of situations, experiences and materials. People can try to assess learning projects in these terms, setting pleasant experiences against unpleasant ones, and comparing the pleasures of learning with the alternative activity which is sacrificed.

• **Brownie points** is a figurative way of referring to benefits which people get from knowing that they are proving their worth, both to themselves and to others. These are the benefits of specific self-esteem.[20] They are immensely important in the motivation model. It is as if people give themselves self-congratulatory marks for good performance in these terms, which are greatly valued. Short of life or death, most people value their sense of self-worth above almost all other considerations.

Somebody's 'winner self' may, for example, be an important aspect of self-image – perhaps because, in childhood, parental praise was conditional on competitive success. A learning course geared to competitive performance can allow this image to be confirmed or dented. The learner will set a standard for personal performance such as "must come top of the class" as part of their motivational assessment, and form expectations about the value of meeting the standard. In this context, the subjective value aspect is in focus (the probability aspect is part of self-efficacy). It is as if the would-be learner expects to win or lose Brownie points, reflecting the gap between expectation and the standard. To some degree the value can be manipulated by altering the difficulty of the standard. But too much adjustment will diminish the value of each Brownie point. The target standard has to be one to be proud of – not one for softies. An individual may have a large number of different aspects of the salient self which can be scored for Brownie points value in this way, ranging, for example, across altruism, creativity, friendship, power, and conformity to group stereotype.

Flow, pleasure, and Brownie points are all vital parts of the picture of total net value. The implications are that:

• a major objective for learning programmes should be to contrive opportunities for learners to experience flow. This powerful motivating force needs to be more widely recognised, and its occurrence monitored as part of the feedback to those who design and offer learning programmes, and who provide guidance or coaching for learners;

• if, despite learning providers' best intentions, learning offers a distasteful or uncomfortable experience, learners will be tempted to spend their time and money on more reliable forms of consumption instead;

• if learning bruises learners' self-image, by whatever means, their motivation for learning will hang by a thread. Maybe only external rewards will bear it up, and perhaps not even that, if the thought of being bribed bruises self-image still further.[21]

So these three elements really matter for motivation. Whether they are assessed in depth out of knowledge, or whether they are assessed by appealing to past, possibly painful, memories of learning, matters correspondingly;[22] and, as before, saliency and stage of learning will also leave their mark.

Motivational assessment
We now look at the nature of the motivational assessment process as a whole, picking up the four themes of Chapter 2 to see how they relate to the value-probability model at project level.

Value and the goal hierarchy
A key point is to see how assessments of external and internal net value at project level relate to higher level goals.

> One of Marie's high level goals is to be a good role model for Zoe as a 21st century woman, and she currently has several intermediate goals which interpret and support this: being willing to learn new things; making a success of my nursing career; being active in the village community.

The net value of learning such as Marie's computer course, can be seen as the net value of the contribution which the project makes to higher goals. This becomes a chain, starting with the bits of net value achieved towards intermediate goals, which in their turn become net value towards the relevant high level goals. This chain is built up by looking at spillover effects on other goals and projects, as well as the effects on the immediate project. All net value must have regard to the alternative scenario which has been sacrificed.

What counts in the end is net value at the level of the highest relevant goals. For Marie, success as a role model would be one of the high level goals where project value is collected. To count the net value for intermediate goals as well would be to double count, so all intermediate value drops out.

> Marie's computer course will help towards her intermediate goal, to show Zoe how learning can help towards major life goals, and how women can develop careers around a family. These are important in showing Zoe how women can manage their lives in the 21st century. But there are disadvantages too. In the same part of Marie's goal hierarchy, the course will take up time which she might otherwise have used for community work. What is more, the learning might have an impact on other high level goals, such as being a good daughter in terms of regular visits to her mother. These have to be brought into the balance as well.

High level goals are not self-justified. They are themselves adopted because they offer value. In the last analysis their value has to be interpreted, as proxies for general satisfaction. This can take two forms: consumption as physical satisfaction and well being; and the value that individuals derive from confirming to themselves and others that they are a particular sort of person – successful, powerful, loving, clever, sensitive, artistic, spiritual – whatever it might be.

The fact that high level goals can be seen as proxies for generalised satisfaction has a further implication. It is not necessary to trace all net value upwards, following the chain to the high level goals. Some of the net value can simply be taken as satisfaction at the project level. If, for example, an episode of learning is enjoyable or absorbing in terms of flow, it can be valued directly for what it does in satisfying basic needs and desires, not for what it may or may not do towards high level goals.

Net value which is referred to higher goals is, perhaps, more likely to come under the external category, while internal value will tend to be valued more immediately. This is where self-esteem Brownie points often come in. It is possible to have intermediate or high level goals relating to Brownie points; but, if there are no such goals, or if such goals are not always in focus, feelings of improved or damaged self-esteem can be valued directly as a consumption benefit. It does not matter whether value is referred upwards or not, or even that it may be split between the two approaches, just so long as all the net value which the person chooses to recognise is brought into the overall judgement of net value.

Saliency

Little has been said so far about what happens when saliency is switched from one self to another. The story here begins with memories, information, rules, expectations, imaginings, and generalisations. These are stored and accessed through separate but interlinked areas of the brain.[23] Verbal content is stored in some areas, while content which is non-verbal – and which therefore remains below the level of rational awareness – is likely to be stored in other

areas. As far as motivation is concerned, it does not matter much what is stored where, so long as it is well linked up.

The stored material is thought to be connected in groups of linked associations, called schemata (plural of schema). These schemata can vary in how close they are to the person's current awareness. Those which are very quickly and easily accessible just spring to mind. These are salient. When we want to access schemata that are more deeply buried, it takes considerable mental effort, and they come into focus only slowly.

Not surprisingly, schemata concerning selves are key in making connections. A self-schema is where a person stores all manner of material about that particular self. When we make a particular self salient, its self-schema comes to the forefront of awareness, while other self-schemata drop into the background. Such shifts can happen in response to extraneous events; or they may be made by individuals themselves, subconsciously or by an act of will.

Bella saw some short television programmes about mentoring in the workplace. Remembering how she had been able to help Marie, as a good friend, she suddenly made a link between that and posters she had seen at work, asking for people to train as mentors. She liked the picture of 'me the mentor' that formed in her mind, and decided to make enquiries about the training.

Motivational assessment is generally influenced by saliency in general, and by self-saliency in particular. Two things can happen:

- Saliency change may just affect the content of value and probability judgements in the motivational assessment, including the identification of the sacrificed alternative. In this case the saliency of the self whose views are being assembled does not change. An example of this is where a driver has seen a gory road accident, and for a while afterwards sees danger in road conditions which would normally be quite unthreatening. He plays safe, and overtakes no one. If the degree of mental processing in motivational assessment is low, particular saliency of this sort may leave a marked, but relatively short-lived, impression on motivational energy.

- Saliency change may involve a shift in the currently highlighted self. This will shift the viewpoint of the self acting as judge, as well as bias the evidence which is considered. Each self will judge differently, irrespective of facts or experience; and each self will encode memories etc. differently. Saliency may bring particular memories and inter-pretations to the forefront of the mind, and tuck others out of sight. This is one of the principal ways in which individuals change their motivational settings. One way we may be able to increase our moti-vation is to juggle selves, and look at things from their different points of view. When we do this, we are deliberately switching saliency, to see if the schemata attached to another self makes us feel keener.

Issues in the learning cycle
Chapter 2 showed how motivational assess-ments and mind-set varies at different stages in the learning cycle (see Figure 2.3, page 11). Three aspects of the cycle need closer attention: intending to implement the decision; coping; and reflection.

After a decision is reached, action on the learning may follow immediately, but there may well be a period of planning and/or waiting for any starting conditions to fall into place. The learner may need to find funding, for example, and there may be a delay before a place becomes available on the course. This is like being under starter's orders.[24]

This state of conditional commitment, when things hang fire, can be a source of difficulty. Whether people eventually follow through with their decisions or drop out before starting depends strongly on how efficiently they form practical intentions to implement the decision. Here, efficiency means setting out steps and target achievements which have to be met if the decision is to be im-plemented.[25] Without these the decision can easily go stale.

Research evidence on implementation intentions is very important for understand-ing motivation. Experiments have shown that setting clear stepping stones strongly affects the chances of starting in earnest. This is a key point both for learners, and for supporters who are encouraging others to learn.

> *Marie makes a check list of everything she will have to organise before she can actually start her course. To begin with she will have to get a grant for materials; give in her notice as part-time assistant at the local shop; and renegotiate with her difficult sister the schedule for visiting their mother. To avoid letting things drift, she sticks the list on the fridge door, and tries to tick something off each week.*

If the stepping stones are safely traversed, and learning begins, the implementation mind-set comes fully into play. As the learning proceeds evidence of the learner's performance starts to accumulate. If it is favourable, all well and good. If it is unfavourable, it will tend to be kept at a distance initially, unprocessed and overlooked. However, if the threat of failure becomes a consistent story, a moment usually arrives where looming failure begins to undermine the whole implementation mind-set and reality breaks through.

This is where the coping stage begins for many learners. It involves a rather zigzag journey back to broader motivational processing.[26] The learner will typically go through a number of recognisable stages (see Figure 3.4), but the route can vary widely. There is no necessary order for the various stages; and while some people may go through several, others will manage with just one or two.[27]

The following is a common route:
• an initial stage where the learner is in denial about looming difficulty, and tries to resist a proper reappraisal;
• next, a stage where the learner will be seeking reasons, attributing the blame to various possible factors.[28] Can the onus be pushed away onto external factors, including

bad luck? Or is it a personal failing? And, if so, can it be remedied – by working harder, for example – or is it somehow inescapable, such as being not clever enough?
• then, depending on these attributions, a stage of doing something about it. Here the options range through giving up, going through the motions, making changes, and to redoubling efforts on the original track.

Motivational ructions face the learner during coping stages such as these. If the decision is for a change, the learning cycle starts again at decision point, and a new motivation and intention come into play. If going through the motions is the answer, the action is in effect redefined as damage limitation, and a new low-motivation mind-set will develop. If the learner redoubles efforts, the implementation mind-set is restored, sometimes with a surge of motivation to even greater heights than before.

Marie had a serious hiccup in confidence early on, but Bella came to the rescue. She helped Marie to face up to the issues, and stop pretending that she was not up to it. It was just beginner's nerves. She also set up Marie's e-mailing facility, so her friend could e-mail her for help "before you get all hot and

---

Coping behaviour
• confronting – by fighting back, expressing anger, seeking change
• distancing – by laughing off, minimizing, forgetting, denial
• self control – by hiding feelings, secrecy over difficulties, counting to ten
• seeking support – by talking to someone, finding out more, advice seeking
• accepting responsibility – by self-criticism, taking the blame
• escape / avoidance – by hoping it will go away, seeking miracle, hiding
• problem solving – by redoubled effort, making new plans, fixing the problem
• positive reappraisal – by finding good in the situation, or identifying useful experience

Figure 3.4 Typical coping behaviours

bothered". Marie's confidence recovered and grew rapidly, and she finished the course with little further difficulty.

For individuals, real skills are involved in recognising their own responses and reactions for what they are, in getting help, and in steering towards sensible solutions. In some circumstances the best thing is to stop chasing the unobtainable; but equally there is a lot to be said for getting back to a creative mastery response.[29] Skills in finding good solutions to coping are a particularly important part of the task of motivational assessment. The whole area of assessment skills will be explored in later chapters.

At the end of the learning cycle, the learner sets aside the last remnants of the implementation mind-set, and makes some kind of retrospective assessment. This could be a subliminal affair, serving little further purpose than to confirm emotional memories of the learning experience. Minimal responses of this sort are common. But some people, with an eye to possible lessons for new projects or reconsideration of higher goals, will make a wide ranging, retrospective assessment. This real reflection will be similar in breadth to the one that led to decision and implementation in the first place.

Reflective assessment produces a new sort of virtual motivation, defined in hindsight.[30] Learners commit to memory their best thoughts on the whole experience, from the start right through to applying the new learning in action. This is a very important stage in the motivational story, for such memories strongly condition any future learning which the person may consider, and the associated motivation. Since high motivation tends to enhance the chances of success,

good experience can set a learner on a strong upward path of ever-increasing motivation and success in learning. Similarly, of course, bad experience can set a learner on a steep downward spiral, which rapidly produces a profound resistance to intentional learning. The thoroughness of mental processing involved in the reflection stage has a most important effect on these long-term dynamics, yet it is commonly the most underdeveloped and poorly supported of all learning-related activities.

Mental processing and the emotions
It is becoming clear that the process of motivational assessment is key to understanding motivation itself. Snap judgements tend to lead to flimsy motivation. The more careful and thoroughgoing the assessment, the more our attention has a chance to explore different saliency; to track back to the value associated with high level goals; to take a long-term view; and to identify the vicarious value we all get when we give value to others who are significant in our lives.[31] Such stretching of assessment brings net value into view which would otherwise be forgotten. It will not guarantee higher levels of motivation overall, but it will produce a different, and probably more robust, result.

An important aspect of motivational assessment concerns the emotions. Until recently the study of emotions has been sadly neglected, and it has been very unclear how they fitted in to motivational assessment. It is now thought that emotions are not themselves directly motivating, but are read as evidence of net value which is then assessed in the usual way.[32]

A new theory builds on this.[33] It now links emotion to the goal hierarchy, enabling emotional responses to be better predicted, and allowing their implications for perceived value to be more effectively drawn in the motivational assessment.

According to this theory, every goal in a person's action hierarchy has a standard of performance. If a real performance unexpectedly exceeds the standard of performance expected, beyond a margin of broad tolerance, the subconscious system intervenes with a surge of feeling which the verbal system interprets as joy. This is evolution's way of giving a push to goal adaptation. If the standard is not achieved, beyond a certain margin of tolerance, an unpleasant emotional response sets in. Again this is a signal to adapt performance of goal, and is a basic part of the experience of coping. Just performing well, within the tolerance band around the standard, leads to a neutral emotional response.

At the Sydney Olympics, only a Gold Medal mattered to Steve Backley, the javelin thrower: it was his goal of goals. His first throw was miraculous – a world record! It gave him an incredible emotional high. Then, against all reasonable odds, this was exceeded almost at once by another competitor, with a throw that won the competition. Having briefly – and unexpectedly – anticipated a Gold Medal, Backley took a Silver. His immediate emotional downer was intense, despite having given a performance beyond prior expectation. His standard was to win Gold, and to do it first time round with a record throw was well over standard. Then suddenly losing it pushed him below standard, and the emotional roller coaster took its toll. Anticipation of such effects can sharpen action, but produce brittle motivation. In Steve Backley's case, his continuing persistence at

his sport shows that his long-term motivation is robust, and much more broadly based than winning Gold would imply.

Further influential aspects of assessment
This chapter concludes with a number of further points which are influential in the motivation story.

- **Closure behaviour** – Some people consider issues only to the point of finding the answer they want, or an answer which will satisfy others, when they want it; otherwise, they do not initiate enquiry.[34] This handicaps their motivation. When closure threatens to become a habit of mind, it endangers learning. This is why forms of education which systematically stress the importance of correct answers over critical thinking run counter to the aims of real lifelong learning.

- **Adding up problem** – If different salient selves have different assessments of the same learning, is there a sense in which these separate motivations can add up to a larger overall motivation? If so, extended processing of the alternative motivational views of the various selves could amplify motivation for or against the learning, simply by accumulation. No one appears to have the answer to this question. There is some, as yet, very flimsy evidence that – as one self takes over from another – the mind tends to deflate the views of the rejected self.[35] Too much saliency switching could therefore tend to diminish any accumulation of motivation which otherwise might arise. Our assumption is that it would probably add to motivation if it could be asserted that the same goal was supported by different selves; and, conversely, if the different selves conflict, it probably would inhibit motivation overall. But the effect is not likely to be a simple question of pluses and minuses.

• **Information and advice** – Motivation is often very strongly affected by relevant information and advice.[36] This includes the influence of role models, whose example illustrates the consequences of action. Information can raise motivation, but it can also depress it, depending on the extent of mental processing applied and the implications drawn from it.

• **Skills in learning and in motivational assessment** – Motivational assessments are greatly conditioned by the skills and strategies which a person has, first to carry through the learning and its aftermath effectively, and second to assess learning options at any stage of the learning cycle.[37] Both these are very responsive to good coaching. The more efficient the learning is, the more value the learner can extract, and the higher the probability of their getting optimum value. So motivation will be bolstered, come what may.

• **Looking ahead** – When life is very complicated, people often try not to look very far ahead. They live from day to day, and develop habits of thinking within short time horizons, to protect themselves from depressive thoughts.[38] The effects on learning choices are devastating, because all the investment value of learning is discounted to nothing. An experienced mentor acting as a motivational coach will often usefully challenge such an assessment.

• **Short-cut attitudes, norms, and beliefs**. Although thinking can start from a clean sheet, taking nothing for granted, this involves a lot of mental processing and it risks inconsistency. More often, people appeal in various degrees to stylised beliefs, stereotypes, old saws, socially established 'do's and don'ts', and/or conventional evaluative prejudices. In extreme cases the value which people collect together in their motivational assessments can be a complete collage. Such assessments are crude, but quick and nearly effort-free.[39] Such attitudes are often proudly held and vehemently defended, as part of the self concept, with different sets of them attached to different selves.

The task of advertisers, promoters, spin-doctors and other persuaders is to elbow old attitudes out and to insert others. To the extent that they succeed, people's motivational assessments can be substantially affected. This is the more so if attitudes about motivational assessment itself can be shifted. Consumer attitudes such as, "people like us act on impulse and follow fashion", are strongly promoted by commercial interests seeking to encourage eternally renewable markets, but it makes motivation very vulnerable to manipulation.

• **Transformative learning** – This is learning which enables people to see large portions of their lives and situation fundamentally differently.[40] At the level of the self concept, this can change the whole structure of selves. A new world view may make for wholesale systematic changes – and even the reinterpretation of old memories, in terms of the new concepts. Some people liken this to secular conversion. History shows that if people can come to see the nature of the power struggles grinding down their lives, fatalism and hopelessness can be replaced by an energy that is revolutionary in their lives, if no further.[41] Such learning has the effect of reconstituting motivation root and branch.

Playing around with the self-concept is, of course, a considerable risk at the personal level. If, for example, ideology and its new structures of power take a grip on the individual, learning itself can ossify in the aftermath. Nonetheless, many people – prompted by their sense of entrapment in old attitudes – find the motivation to buy this pig-in-a-poke; and there are many examples of spectacular results.

Notes and references (Numbers refer to publications listed in the Reference section)

[1]   Examples using first names only are fictional.

[2]   See 50 for a useful account of this approach; also 193, 229, 241 & 247.

[3]   See Bandura 10.

[4]   See Weiner 241 for a discussion of the Atkinson model where independence breaks down; also 70.

[5]   See Feather 85 for a general survey.

[6]   Although standard, this contention has not been without its critics. See 215.

[7]   See 215.

[8]   This is discussed in Weiner 241 & Bandura 9.

[9]   The self-efficacy concept is Bandura's major achievement. See 9, 10 & 11.

[10]   See 213.

[11]   See 10.

[12]   See 9 & 10 for a close analysis of these virtuous and vicious circles.

[13]   This is related to Vygotsky's 'zone of proximal development'. See 229 & 236.

[14]   This distinction is due to Bandura. See 9.

[15]   The analysis of attributions has been extended by Weiner (see 240), building on Rotter's internal and external locus of responsibility.

[16]   See Dweck 69 for a full treatment.

[17]   See 176 for economists' concepts of time preference and risk aversion; also 40.

[18]   See Czikszentmihalyi 53.

[19]   See 54.

[20]   See 47, 110, 144, 155, 163, 197 & 205.

[21]   See 235.

[22]   See 146.

[23]   See 144.

[24]   See Gollwitzer & J Barg 104 generally.

[25]   See 107.

[26]   See 24, 127, 129, 134, 144, 159, 162 & 240.

[27]   See 162 for a good survey of coping behaviour by Lazarus.

[28]   See Weiner 240.

[29]   See 24.

[30]   See 114.

[31] See Schroeder et al 210 for an excellent summary of altruism and helping.
[32] See 55 & 56, and an important survey by Ford et al 92.
[33] See 38.
[34] See Kruglanski & Webster 160.
[35] See 137.
[36] See 48 for the motivating effects of good information and guidance.
[37] See 200.
[38] See 100.
[39] See 231 for group efforts on influencing attitude.
[40] See Mezirow 67 & 173.
[41] See Freire 90 for the definitive statement.

Chapter 4:
Motivation for learning strategy

Introduction
This chapter examines the question of motivation for learning in strategic terms: what shapes the motivation for adopting and carrying out general strategies for learning and, in particular, what informs the processes that make people eager to pursue the strategy of lifelong learning through a succession of projects.[1]

Studies of motivation for learning have mainly focused on the project level, and in particular on the experiences of younger children at school. Detailed research into people's learning strategies, and the motivational issues behind them, is lacking. It is necessary therefore to extrapolate very largely from project level experience if we are to construct a plausible picture of strategic motivation to pursue a learning strategy.

Many people reject the idea of a learning strategy as too businesslike in flavour, implying an over-planned approach to everyday action. It hardly chimes with the laid-back spontaneity of popular culture. Yet many such people, who deny that they have a learning strategy, actually do have one of sorts, at some degree of development. It may take the form of a habitual response, largely submerged below the level of consciousness; it may be too private to be declared; it may be in the head rather than on paper or shared with others; it may only

intermittently come into sharp focus. As we have seen, the whole scene is complicated by the switching of action goal hierarchies, with their different priorities and trade offs, according to the switching of salient selves – some selves having little strategy, some having a lot. Even people who persist in denying any sort of strategy may have a negative default strategy – "Catch me doing more learning! I've got my fishing!" – or a tacit strategy, which is real but simply unrecognised.

The question of strategic motivation for learning therefore languishes in denial and obscurity, yet it is very important. A learning strategy is vital in establishing connectivity between episodes of learning, and in bringing a momentum and a pattern to those episodes. It develops the linkages that make the difference between occasional episodes and an efficient ongoing system of personal learning motivation. Without it learning episodes are a random walk, each step no doubt motivated, but having little sense of direction overall. Like a jigsaw puzzle, the full, mature value of acquired knowledge only emerges when its pieces are fitted together.

Strategies for learning
Recognised or otherwise, learning strategies serve different purposes for different people. Figure 4.1 illustrates one branch of an

individual's action hierarchy.[2] This simplified example shows how a person intends to pursue the high level goal of becoming a millionaire by four intermediate goals. These are of two different kinds:

• goals which are about how a person behaves in implementing the high level life goal;
• goals which are about what specific sets of actions need to be done in the world.

Action sets (clustered in the shaded area at bottom right in Figure 4.1) consist of actual or potential projects which implement any particular 'what' intermediate goal, and by doing so help to implement the relevant high level goal(s). A set of projects is not necessarily closed, new items can be invented to go in, and items can be removed or changed. The items may be fully defined, and activated; but often enough they will be possibilities, waiting in the wings. At certain times there may be no clearly specified items at all, just the general heading of the intermediate goal. In the case shown, there are items to do with building financial alliances, and learning projects to implement an intermediate lifelong learning strategy goal associated with becoming a millionaire.

In real life, action hierarchies are rather more complex than this (see Figure 2.1, page 8 for example). The hierarchy will have other branches for different life goals, each with an array of intermediate goals and projects. All the branches will overlap to some extent, establishing trade-offs and complementarities, which all come into the motivational assessment.

A strategy is simply a set of plans or intentions to implement a high level or intermediate goal. Indeed for most purposes the terms strategy and goal are interchangeable. So, to match her goals, our wannabe millionaire has four intermediate strategies and one high level strategy on this branch of her overall action hierarchy.

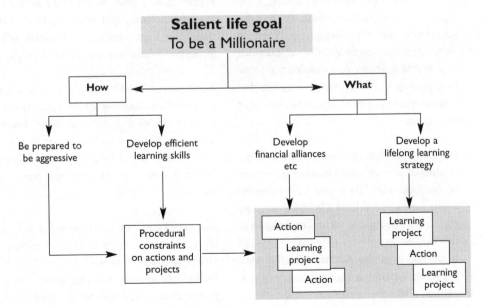

Figure 4.1 The 'to be a millionaire' branch of an action hierarchy

This is just one individual. It is much the same for any person with any sort of learning strategy and higher level learning goals. Whatever the shape of a person's learning strategies under a particular salient self, a diagram similar to Figure 4.1 could be drawn to illustrate them. This highlights a number of points:

- There is no reason why learning, and in particular some form of lifelong learning, should not be a very high level life goal in its own right. This seems rare in real life, because people mostly learn for goals other than learning. But such a goal and a high level strategy to carry it out is possible, and makes a lot of sense.

- More commonly, a learning strategy will be defined at intermediate level, and there may be more than one of them, each intended to contribute towards a different high level goal.

- An intermediate learning strategy, as Figure 4.1 shows, can relate to a 'how' goal. Here, our millionaire-to-be vows to develop good learning skills in pursuing intermediate action goals under the same high level goal, and takes steps to see that the various actions and projects are run in that spirit.

- The idea of an intermediate learning strategy relating to a 'what' goal, i.e. concrete action, is also common. The would-be millionaire might, for example, have a learning strategy to 'learn all about the technologies used in the production of an extensive range of trade goods in the business'. In this case the items would match each technological element in the product range, as it expands over time.

- A learning project can appear as an item under any intermediate strategy which is relevant. Where there is an intermediate learning strategy it will tend to have a concentration of learning projects, but may also include other relevant actions. Figure 4.1 shows a learning project under 'financial alliances'; and under the intermediate learning strategy there is an action goal, such as 'maintain internet facilities to support web-based learning'. This means that not all learning is brigaded under learning strategy, nor does a learning strategy consist only of learning projects.

An individual could, therefore, have learning strategies (plural) in all these forms at the same time, and divide learning projects across these and other strategies in quite complex ways. A person with a high level lifelong learning goal, for example, could also have as a procedural intermediate goal, 'to support other people's lifelong learning', and at the same time have the intermediate action goal, 'always to be engaged on one learning project, and have another in the pipeline'. That makes two intermediate strategies inside one high level strategy.

More generally, an individual may have some intermediate learning strategies, relating to some high level goals, and these learning strategies may not be consistent across the action hierarchy. If this happens, motivation for one piece of learning may be at the expense of another.

An important lesson emerges from this. If we want a deeper understanding of strategic motivation we must explore how individuals spread learning over the goal hierarchies which belong to their various salient selves.

Lifelong learning strategies

Lifelong learning strategies, whether intermediate or high level, are a particular concern here. They can take a number of different forms, and Figure 4.2 shows how they can vary.[3]

Three key aspects of learning, as shown in Figure 4.2 are: the distinction between proactive and reactive; the choice between general and specific learning objectives; and the spectrum between intermittent and continuous.

• A reactive learning strategy sets conditionals such as:"I will do some learning – if and when X happens." A common example of this is the decision many busy people make to read a substantial book when they go on a holiday, because they are normally too busy to do it. The trouble with this is that not on holiday means no substantial reading. A proactive learning strategy does not set conditionals. An intention such as, "I'll arrange my life so I can keep myself up to date with the reading I want to do", would be proactive.

• A specific learning strategy is closely targeted on a particular topic or field of learning. "I am going to learn all there is about old clocks", would seem to many people to be a specific strategic objective. This can be compared with a more general strategy, "I'm a general antiquarian, and I like to learn about any kind of old artefact or writing that takes my fancy."

• A continuous learning strategy might amount to, "I'll make sure I've got at least one learning project on the go at any time." This would contrast with an intermittent strategy to learn at intervals such as, "I aim to do an Open University module every X years."

Motivation processes for learning strategies

All this helps us to define and position the idea of a learning strategy, and in particular a lifelong learning strategy. But we shall need to explore the motivation which attaches to any learning strategy. What is it, and where does it come from? Why do people put effort into their strategies?

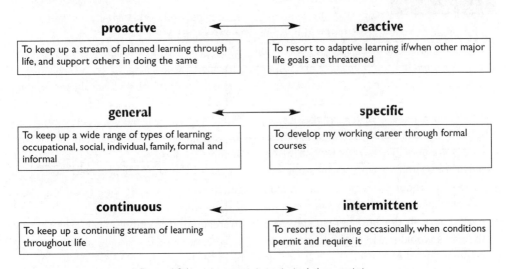

proactive ←——————→ **reactive**	
To keep up a stream of planned learning through life, and support others in doing the same	To resort to adaptive learning if/when other major life goals are threatened

general ←——————→ **specific**	
To keep up a wide range of types of learning: occupational, social, individual, family, formal and informal	To develop my working career through formal courses

continuous ←——————→ **intermittent**	
To keep up a continuing stream of learning throughout life	To resort to learning occasionally, when conditions permit and require it

Figure 4.2 Learning strategies: principal characteristics

There are two steps. First we define strategic motivation in the same way as was done for learning projects, as keenness producing energy. Second, we hold that strategic motivation is produced, as it was at project level, from a process of internal assessment.

The question is: where to go from there within this broad framework? At project level, we used three other fundamental concepts to explore motivation: the learning cycle, the salient self, and the value/expectancy model. All these can be applied at strategic level, and if they were, it would imply little or no difference in principle between motivational processes at the two levels. If valid, this is both appealing and simplifying. More importantly, if it were not so, there would be major inconsistencies in action. This, then, is a reasonable place to start, when faced with only the most slender evidence from research, and it is the position taken here.

The strategic cycle
Figure 4.3 shows how, at the project reflection stage, the learner compares the outcomes of a completed learning project with what is still needed under intermediate learning goals not yet achieved. What may impel the person into interest in yet another project under the same intermediate goal is the motivational energy for the higher strategy. But if that motivation is ebbing or coming to an end, a reappraisal of the strategy can set in. This has its own cycle, with initial interest, pre-decision assessments, decision, implementation and reflection stages – very much the same pattern as at project level, only paced differently.

A small scale diagram of a project-level learning cycle appears in the bottom right corner of Figure 4.3. For simplicity only a single such cycle is shown, but individuals

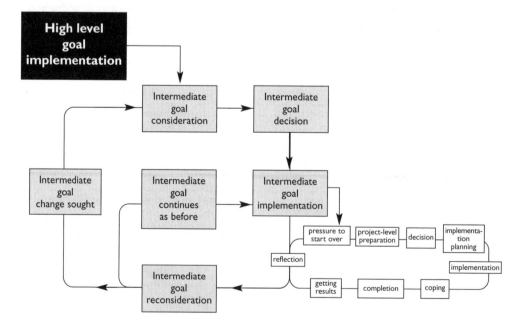

Figure 4.3 Reflection

are likely to have several cycles, each with their own project, in progress at the same time, and each possibly at a different stage. These are all tied into a revision cycle of intermediate-level strategy, itself prompted by implementation of a high level goal.

When learners are reflecting on the outcome of a particular learning project, they may simply decide to press ahead with the next project, taking the intermediate strategy further. But they could take time out to reflect on any intermediate goal changes which might be needed in the light of their project experience. In rare cases they might even reconsider the high level goal at the top of the hierarchy. In this way the flow of reflections on projects can trigger strategic rethinking. A serious failure on a project may be enough to cause that to happen. But quite often the experience of projects will build up over a period, and the move to a serious strategic reappraisal is slow and cumulative.

If a learner's reflections on this build-up of project evidence simply confirm the strategy, the lessons learned are ploughed back into new or other current projects. A project may have been completed successfully enough in terms of what is achieved, but there could be a failure on a constraining objective relating to how it went. Our millionaire, for instance, may have succeeded in the learning, but may not have shown enough power in her dealings. She may deduce from this that she needs to be more assertive in the next project.

If some changes are needed in the intermediate goal(s), project level activity may be put on hold or on a care-and-maintenance basis, until the changes are made, and their consequences for projects worked through.

The cycle of intermediate strategy adjustment is itself set inside a further similar adjustment cycle, this time centred on the highest life goal level in the action structure (not shown in Fig 4.3). The time lags before those highest life goals are shifted can be very long indeed. Revisions may be turned over only once or twice in a lifetime, unless radical shifts in life experience or situation intervene.

It seems to be a standard part of the action hierarchy that strategic revision at any of these higher levels is only triggered when lower-level experience exceeds a tolerance band.[4] If either success or failure passes the limits often enough, or severely enough in a single instance, the learner will start a reappraisal at the next level up. The tolerance bands are normally shadowy and only loosely defined, and may even be invented as activity proceeds. Yet the degrees of tolerance are very important for understanding strategic reappraisal. Research is needed to establish what tolerance bands apply, and then to see how long it takes to push through a reappraisal, and what happens to lower level activity in the meanwhile.

The higher up the hierarchy that goals are revised, the more difficult and costly revision becomes. Changing a higher level goal means rethinking a correspondingly larger slice of life. This requires great effort and may involve painful writing-off of past goals, and reappraisal of time and energy invested in activity. This is why time lags in strategy revision are long, and why the tolerances which trigger revision are set so wide. It also explains why strategies are often described in vague terms in the first place.

Motivation during the strategic cycle
The strategic cycle, at whatever level, has its

own processes of motivational assessment, which we take broadly to follow those which operate at project level. If a new or changed strategy appears to be needed, this will be assessed and a decision will be reached. The decision leads to implementation plans, and at a certain point to implementation. As this process unfolds, motivation for the strategic intention changes from a virtual form to something real. At project level, the cycle can be seen as a succession of mind-sets, culminating in an implementation mind-set which is very distinctive;[5] in the under-researched field of strategy variation, it is not clear whether there are such distinctive mind-set differences.

At some point after implementation of the strategic goal begins, evidence will begin to arrive from projects or other sources. If this threatens strategic failure, the learner will come to a coping stage, where emotions will be negative, and the fate of the strategy will hang in the balance. At such a point, the psychology of coping would appear to apply just as it does at project level. Any implementation mind-set will be set aside, temporarily at least, and coping responses will begin, running through a number of stages, not necessarily in standard order.

A typical sequence might be as follows:[6]

1. Denying the need for revision: "I can always improve things"; "It's unlikely to happen again – it was just bad luck/a one-off". Having to accept that something has gone amiss may be damaging to personal reputation and costly to put right.

2. Distancing from the issue: "Things have gone wrong, but it's not my business"; "The boss may need to do something, but not me".

3. Procrastinating over what changes might be made: "It's all more difficult than it looks – there are so many things that might be done"; "I won't be able to see it clearly until X happens – one thing at a time".

4. Going through the motions: "I've just got to put up with it"; "I'm keeping my head down".

5. Collapse of confidence (the learned helplessness response): "I give up! I'm washing my hands of the whole thing! They really shouldn't expect me to cope with this."

6. Resolving to return to the charge (the mastery response): chastened by experience, but more determined than ever to make strategy revisions and then to make the strategy stick at lower level, "I will have another crack at it! I'm not going to let it beat me". This approach would refresh any implementation mind-set.

Individuals' motivation to adopt and implement learning strategies therefore varies as the strategic cycle unfolds. If in the end a strategy is rejected in favour of something else, there will probably be a tendency to blacken its reputation in memory: "I knew there was something bad about it all along...". This self-justificatory approach interprets the fact of change as evidence of the former strategy's own demerit.

This cycle at strategy level has some important general features. For example:

• Tolerance of large scale inconsistency: It takes a lot of effort to get everything lined up. Each salient self has its own characteristic goal hierarchy. This is likely to cause turbulence and inconsistency in goals, if identity and saliency changes radically.

- Large scale overlap between different branches of the action hierarchy: Projects may do multiple duty under several strategic objectives, of varying importance to the individual. Revision of projects, or revision of the higher strategy guiding projects, is perhaps most likely to reflect the most immediately relevant goal strategy. But it is almost as likely to be an indirect spill-over from strategic revision elsewhere in the hierarchical structure. This means that strategic motivation for learning may be as much at risk from failings in other parts of the learner's life as it is from failings in learning projects and strategy.

- Widespread helplessness: Reflecting the overlap, coping behaviour can spread from one area of a person's life to another. People who are in great trouble – through profound grief or shock, for example – may lose motivation all round and opt out of goal-directed action altogether. If this happens they often fall back on 'business as usual' behaviour, keeping to familiar routines and self-narratives, and living from day-to-day. It may require a great passage of time, or some form of transformative learning, to put this right.

- Socially determined strategies at every goal level: Cultural assumptions, conventional wisdom and social rules-of-thumb are passed on from person to person, and from generation to generation, because they have stood the test of time. Studies of important life goals across population samples show very strong conventional patterning, often shaped by stage of life.[7] Revision of learning strategies may well be

inhibited if it would mean cutting across these strong currents of practice. Hiding in conventional patterns can be an efficient short term way of dealing with what would be a huge task for each individual, but it is doubtful if it pays off in the longer run.

- Vague goals: Strategic goals and strategies may start life unobtrusively, as cultural norms or beliefs, or habitual practice, or as interpretations drawn from projects which a person has just fallen into by chance. But they may simply spring from formless beginnings, just as fully sophisticated language develops from infant burbling. There is a good case for improving on such strategies, which may not be the product of the rational, top-down process described earlier.

Probability and value
In general, the analysis of motivational processes for learning at project level can be applied also to learning strategies. The motivation for a strategy, whether of learning or anything else would therefore be related to the perception of net value and the probability of getting that value, and Figure 3.1, page 19 would remain broadly relevant. But there is a different feel about motivation at the strategic level.

People may not talk very much about their learning strategies. Having the distant big picture always in view has a cost, because there is a lot of thinking to do, and also because any doubts about that picture might demotivate action at the project level.

We saw in Chapter 3 that engaging an implementation mind-set tidied away doubt about the wider value of a learning project. This includes the validity of the strategic goals underwriting the net value of the project. So a lifelong learner will not constantly revisit the strategic goals of lifelong learning, however they are expressed. When projects are going fast and furious strategies sink into the dim light, like half-forgotten narratives, with low saliency, more like tacit self-knowledge than anything else.

But this does not mean that motivation to develop and implement strategies, when awakened, is itself a low level experience. Quite the reverse. People voluntarily engaged in transformative learning at the strategy level commonly report powerful feelings of renewed motivation.[8] Responding to the basic need for personal autonomy, the sense of control which reaffirmed strategy can give produces deep satisfaction.[9] Life without strategy is chaotic, and chaos is demotivating.

Probability – On the probability side of the strategic motivational process, self-efficacy and means-ends beliefs will again be important in the story.

Self-efficacy has two aspects as before, one in strategic assessment and one in successful implementation of a strategy. People will embark more keenly upon revision of the projects they undertake, if they are confident of their ability to examine them objectively (for failure as well as for success) and to reach useful conclusions. If they can call on coaching support, or get help through transformative learning courses, so much the better.

But the ability to do strategic motivational assessment would not be enough by itself. The next question is: "If I can implement my strategy properly, what are the chances of winning out?" The stronger the answer to this question, the keener the individual is

likely to be to pursue the chosen strategy. Poverty, and the lack of good experience in carrying through strategy, can be fundamental barriers. If so-called fecklessness is the fruit of low self-efficacy for strategic issues, fatalism about strategy is the killer disease lurking in the wake of poverty and social exclusion.[10]

Value – On the net value side of the motivational equation are intrinsic and extrinsic considerations.

• Intrinsic satisfactions. These derive from the basic human need for control through autonomy, but also from the satisfaction of other basic needs – such as finding meaning in a complex world, the need for a competent grasp of the environment, and being accepted by others.

• Inauthenticity: According to Deci and Ryan's theory of self determination, much personal strategy feels inauthentic to those who pursue it, and may seem inauthentic to others as well.[11] This is because the strategy refers to values and goals relating to partially separate self-concepts, which have grown up as life unfolds, and not to the true self. The unpleasant feeling of inauthenticity can be regarded as a failing of self-esteem relating to the true self. It is a wake-up call prompting the individual to make the true self salient, and to conduct a thorough strategic audit on that basis. Challenging this inauthenticity is the particular purpose of transformative learning. It can be very costly to individual peace of mind, but the solutions it may eventually bring can be more powerfully motivating than almost any other experience.

• State of flow: The sense of rightness and

harmony which exists when a person achieves and implements a broad, considered stability and balance in the goal hierarchy, both at strategic and project levels, can be a flow-like phenomenon.[12] It is deeply rewarding for those lucky enough to experience it.

• Extrinsic rewards: Long term studies show that people who, as college students, had a strong strategic grip on ordering their life goals had very definite rewards:[13] they lived longer; were healthier than less organised contemporaries; and were more successful in their careers.

• Employment: In an increasingly flexible labour market, employers favour employees who can act strategically and keep learning.

• Coping with uncertainty: Generally, good strategists can react creatively and in a timely fashion to the gross uncertainties which afflict modern economies, social communities and family life.

Little research has been conducted on the way that people weigh up net value and probability to produce the degree of enthusiasm required to adopt and carry through a strategy. The leading hypothesis (based on the expectancy/valency theory examined in Chapter 3) would be that they are combined multiplicatively to produce strategic motivation. But this is rather more in doubt than at project level. The multiplicative formulation may not apply if strategic value is derived strongly from acting out of a sense of obligation, or if it is oriented towards avoidance of punishment, including self punishment.[14] Avoidance is where a person does not so much wish to achieve goals as aim to lessen the risk of non-achievement.[15]

An example of acting from a sense of obligation would be where a member of a religious community thinks that there should be a daily ritual of learning from sacred texts as a key intermediate learning strategy. The devotee's motivation to do this is not responsive to increases in expected value or to probability expectations about getting it. It has an absolute quality about it, as if keenness is somehow overtaken by compulsion. Here, indeed, there may be more than just a doubt about the multiplicative form, motivation may not even be an increasing function of value or probability at all. Such motivation needs more study.

Whatever the functional form, the nature of the assessment process in producing motivation at the strategic level remains important, alongside the effects of saliency, level and stage. Much carries over from the project level discussion of this. But, at the strategic level, three personality factors need to be stressed: futurity, mastery and normative personality orientations. All express themselves in assessment.

• **Futurity** is the personality factor of far-sightedness.[16] This captures the way in which – allowing for salient self and context – people appear to differ over the time horizons they use for considering goals and strategies. Some people do not look beyond next week, others may think in generations. This affects strategy thinking. The process of strategic formulation and revision takes place over extended periods, and the chance is high that a learner's assumptions affecting net value will fail, or will have to be changed radically, before they can fully carry through their strategies. The truncation of the time horizon in strategic assessment will have

very important motivational consequences, not least in cutting out all the
values associated with long term conservation and sustainability. Learning
strategies are just as vulnerable to chaos
as other strategies, whether it arises in the
external world of events or in the internal
world of the emotions. A change to a
chaotic environment – such as in the
Kosovo crisis, or in a strong emotional response to sudden bereavement, for example
– can cause time horizons to foreshorten
rapidly and dramatically. Motivation at the
level of personal strategy can collapse into
mere day-to-day survival mode.

• **Mastery orientation**, refers to learners who
are highly likely to respond with resilience
and renewed effort to the first signs of
possible failure. They tend to stick to strategy and to seek to make it work by
greater effort, or at least finding positive
ways to revise it. They do not act as if
under a cloud of disapproval. This
mastery response correlates well with
high and robust motivation.[17]

• **Normative orientation**, in contrast, refers
to learners who are highly bound by rules
and obligations.[18] For such people, studies
appear to show a tendency towards anxiety
in failure situations, as if they are pro-
grammed to expect punishment. In coping
behaviour at the strategy level, such people will tend to bottle out, with motivation
collapsing and strategy being abandoned.

Notes and references (Numbers refer to publications listed in the Reference section)

[1] For a discussion of the definition of a lifelong learning strategy see Smith & Spurling 220.
[2] See 38 for a discussion of goal hierarchy.
[3] For discussions of the meaning of lifelong learning see Smith & Spurling 220, Ranson 196 & Coffield 45.
[4] See 38; also 30.
[5] See 105 & 127.
[6] See 162.
[7] See 127; also 128 for general background.
[8] See Freire 90; also 222.
[9] See 30.
[10] See Bandura 10.
[11] For an example see 152; also 126 & 202
[12] See 53 & 54.
[13] Information contributed by Jim Welsh at a research workshop, source not identified.
[14] See 215.
[15] See 74 & 75.
[16] See 40 for a comprehensive review of time preference, and Gjesme 100 for futurity.
[17] See 134.
[18] See 133 & 134.

Chapter 5:
Developing learning motivation in the family

Introduction

The first four chapters have explored motivation as a mental process based on assessment – an intensely personal activity. As this process unfolds within individuals it is shaped by, and helps to shape, the wider social and physical world. Four social environments have particular influence on learning motivation at project and at strategy level: the family; educational institutions and the professions involved in them; communities; and the world of work.

• **Family is** taken here to be the relational and domestic context where children are reared, and/or where people who are intimately involved in each others lives on a long-term basis share resources and support each other in daily living.[1] Families vary widely in form and scope, and very often include people who are not related or linked by marriage. We use the word family here as a generic term only, and not with any one particular model in mind. The term reflects ideals of lifelong commitment, affection, responsibility and care, balanced in different ways in different cultures, and achieved with differing degrees of success and failure.

• **Learning context** here includes the whole of the supply side of the learning market. It includes, as a major part, all initial education in institutions up to and including university level.

• **Community** is the whole array of social groupings, other than family and kin. Membership of such groups is a recognised part of the person's group identity.[2] A young black male, for example, may be psychologically committed as a member of: a specific ethnic group; a local residential community; a group of friends; a church, chapel or mosque; a college class; a protest group and so on. Membership of these groups overlap, and the young man may change his membership of them from time to time. Group identity responds to 'we', rather than 'I'. It is that part of the (salient) self-concept which relates to the groups that individuals belong to, and whose general attributes they accept as an aspect of their individual identity.

• **Work place** (in this context) means the environment, other than the family and the social community, where a person earns income in exchange for work.[3] In many ways it is part of the social community, but we consider it separately here, because it has particular implications in the motivation story. Where people work without pay inside the family, or voluntarily in the community, that is included under those headings.

Figure 5.1 shows how these environments interlace and overlap. They each influence motivation to learn directly, but at the same time the effect of any one of them is dependent on all the others. To be effective, motivational policy and practice need to recognise the cat's cradle of forces at work in this system, influencing both motivation for particular actions and goals, and also personal motivational development (shown at the centre).

Within Figure 5.1 the influence exerted by each environment is related to the influencing skills of people in that environment, and their motivation to apply those skills. At the same time, their particular influence is modified by the interplay of forces among all the influencers, elbowing in here or lending weight there (as shown by the dotted line). Having both the will and the skill to influence

motivation is crucial for all the influencing parties, as they seek to lever individual motivation by applying their weight in the cat's cradle. The following chapters consider various factors underpinning the activities and motivation of these influencers.

We begin with the family, in many respects the cornerstone of influence on individual motivation. This chapter covers relevant aspects of nurture and personal development, and Chapter 6 looks at the family's wider influencing activities.

• Personal development concerns the way that families help their members to develop in motivation. Although this is mainly about young people and their nurture, it is not exclusively so. It is generally thought that

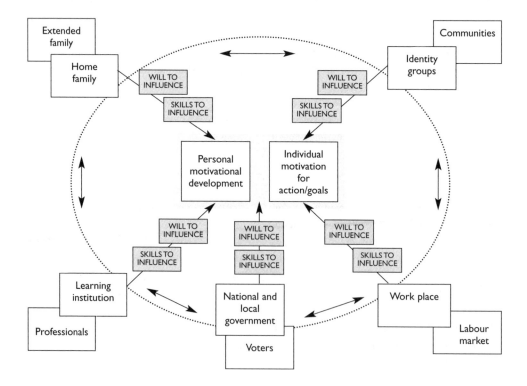

Figure 5.1   The cat's cradle of motivational forces

individuals' motivational processes gain their unique settings in early years, and that these are broadly maintained in later years. This is why societies are so deeply concerned in supporting the development of children's motivation. But research and general experience show that motivational settings and processes are not completely fixed by early adulthood. They remain susceptible to significant change throughout life. This raises real possibilities for increasing motivation for learning in adulthood.

• The wider influencing activities of the family are about the way that the family context influences, and is influenced by, the motivational knowledge, processes and skills of family members.

Developing the motivational processes
In describing the natural history of the process producing mature motivation, within the family, we follow well established theory. This holds that – across cultures and classes – people are broadly similar in the psychological systems producing motivation, but that every person's own motivation system has a unique setting reflecting genetic inheritance and individual experience. Families create the first, and very largely shape the second in early years. The theory implies that, even if the input of information could be the same between one person and another (which in practice it never can be), the output in terms of motivation for any intended action or goal would not necessarily be equivalent. The family has a key role in initiating the settings.

Psychological research shows that the broad framework of motivational processes gradually crystallizes out over childhood.[4] Like other development, it happens more quickly

for some people than for others, and it can be impeded or damaged in particular cases. In this respect it is closely associated with the acquisition of language. Motivation is very largely a product of the verbal mind, and it cannot stretch beyond the margins of awareness built into a person's language skills. The genes appear to create a disposition towards the use of structured language, which nurture and social interaction draws out. It is much the same story for motivation.

Infancy
New-born infants are verbally unaware. Chapter 2 highlighted the strong basic needs which direct and energize their initial learning and psychological development. The main needs which concern us here are competence, affiliation and autonomy, taken as an interlocking trio; and, as a background to these, the general principle which directs humans to avoid danger and pain, and to maximise pleasure and security.[5] These basic needs are hardwired into the brain by evolution; expressed through the genes, as drawn out by experience and environment; and supported by the individual's emotional system. The individual experiences positive feelings if the needs are satisfied, and negative feelings if they are not. Without these basic needs, infants would be unable to come to terms with the world. They would not be able to acquire language and, with it, the advanced mental functions which support the hierarchy of conscious goals and actions.

The expression and satisfaction of these basic needs in infancy is therefore a crucial first step, not only for survival but also for learning, and ultimately for building a self-aware motivational system. The unfolding of this whole process depends heavily on parents and other nurturing adults in the family environment. The nurturing role is largely instinctive and gene-driven, but relies on the adults' conscious and subconscious memories of their own nurture, and that of others within the family group. Nurturers will normally follow their instincts in trying to create an environment which is constantly adapting and changing to awaken and draw out the effects of the genes. This nurturing intention can be voluntarily extended to non-genetic members of the family, such as fostered, adopted or step-children.

Infants will learn less well, and may become inhibited in the expression of their basic needs, to the extent that the environment is chaotic. The damage resulting from that can be lifelong and very difficult (though not impossible) to remedy, because its effects are written into the schemata of the subconscious mind. Temporary inhibitions and frustrations will leave no lasting scars, if nurturers can offer predictable and consistent responses to infants' exploratory and manipulative gambits – such as the notorious rages of the two-year old.

The effects of these very early environments carry right through into the verbally-based motivational processes developed through maturity. They appear close to the surface in much of the intrinsic side of net value: the joy of new meanings (competence); the self-esteem aspects of Brownie points (autonomy and affiliation); and the experience of flow (autonomy). If expression of the underlying genetic prompting is seriously inhibited – by religious or educational diktat for example – individuals will have difficulty in realising personal value in these key areas.

Childhood/adolescence
Once the threshold of language is crossed, the verbal concepts and cognition necessary for motivational assessments, which produce changes in conscious motivational energy, become progressively more developed.[6]

Young children with the basics of language are initially only concerned with learning projects in the here and now. They are motivated principally by the immediate experience of intrinsic values of pleasure and flow. They also tend to see value in black and white terms – "Really good!" or "Very bad!" It takes time for their assessment of net value to become more nuanced.

Very young children's sense of self is not clearly differentiated from that of the nurturer. The notion of the separate self develops only gradually in the early years, as children impute characteristics to themselves from the reactions of the people around them. Those reactions – rejection or a conditionality in affection, in particular – can have very marked effects. The process of individuation accelerates later when, in pre-adolescent years, older children begin to make vigorous social comparison between themselves and others, notably their peers.[7] The mid-teens brings experimentation, where different identities are donned and doffed like so many hats.[8] As the self-concept clarifies, it begins a process of partial differentiation, producing in due course the multifaceted identity of the mature adult, explored in Chapter 2.

The motivational implication is clear. The 'Brownie points' element, which is a major motivational feature for older children and most adults, can only develop in pace with the establishment of personal identities. It takes time for considerations of self-esteem to emerge. In the turbulence of establishing identity, the focus of young people's self-esteem will change frequently, often swinging from one extreme to the other and using the family as a sounding board for response.

On the probability side of the account, the evidence is that young children initially have no learning inhibitions on the grounds of incapacity: they think they can do anything.[9] They cannot clearly separate personal efficacy from external factors, such as luck. Also, importantly for motivation, they initially make no distinction between innate ability and effort. If learning fails they will often show no interest in identifying the cause, being content to put it down to unknown causes.

This innocence erodes over time, as children try to gauge their identity and capacity by comparing their own performance with other people's, and picking up from the judgements of people around them. Labels such as clever or lazy or thick are readily taken to heart, prompted by the overt expression or withdrawal of approval by parents and teachers, and from the comments of peers. If taken into the self-concept, such entity beliefs can have a powerful influence for motivation to learn throughout life.[10] Negative labels can be devastating. Although they can be altered, they are very resistant to efforts to shift them. The notion that personal capacities may be irrevocably limited (commonly believed about IQ for instance) can push failing learners into helplessness, with nowhere left to go.

Overall, taking value and probability together,

the depth of understanding which children bring to bear in motivational assessments reflects growth in their capacity to generalise on experience and to play out imagined scenarios. Experience of learning success and failure provides a rich school for motivational processes. But play is also fundamental, because it enables experience to be stretched many-fold through imagination and thought-experiment.

Quite naturally, project motivation develops first, and the processes of strategy motivation come as one of the very last stages in the developmental process.[11] Younger children are natural adherents to the idea of jumping a fence when you get to it, and tend to take learning tasks as presented. Strategic learning action only begins to make sense as mental range and experience approach full growth, nurtured by success. Sadly, some people never get that far.

Developing motivation in adulthood
The development process begins to slow down in the mid-teens, and stabilises substantially by the early 20s.[12] Some believe that this crystallizing leads to a fixed learning identity, which, once formed, cannot be undone or shifted. There is no substantial body of evidence to support this dangerous, but popular, myth. On the contrary, it is clear from wide experience that transformative learning can shift important parts of the self-concept involved in motivational processing, at any stage of life; and that motivational coaching can permanently change the habits and skills involved in motivational assessment, for young and old alike. Motivation is not an unalterable feature, like height or hat size, which people become stuck with as the consequence of development. The process can be tuned up to higher pitches of efficiency

and knowledge for more or less any age and circumstance, and it often is.

For many young people entering adulthood, the upshot of earlier development is unsatisfactory. Just as they can emerge from childhood with poor language skills, in much the same way their personal motivational system may be to a degree immature or damaged. In these terms there are different forms of motivational immaturity, just as there is illiteracy in reading, writing and speaking.

Many people are, for example, deficient in strategic thinking. Some young adults are handicapped by an excessive sensitivity to performance testing. Others may be afflicted by unduly low self-efficacy, and be unable to sort out the difference between low self-efficacy and fatalism about means and ends. Not only that, they may well have developed superficiality and habituation in assessment and attributions. Such defects are likely to have adverse effects on the learning motivation, leaving these young people very vulnerable to external influence. If they cannot clarify their own goals and actions, they are faced with constantly trying to do things to satisfy other people's (often conflicting) requirements, or to giving up and dropping out altogether.

A plateauing in motivational development seems to overtake most people in adult life, although it is far from inevitable that it should. There is still room for two major developmental factors, both biological in origin and both expressed within the family: parenthood, and grandparenthood.

Parenthood and nurture
Parenthood, as an intimate relationship, is a transformative learning experience of major

dimensions.[13] Studies show earthquake-like effects on psychological personality measures, values, salient self-concepts, and behaviour patterns of the vast bulk of people who become parents for the first time and who are closely involved in the care of their infant.

The nurturing response is triggered by involvement, and the effect seems to be weaker in fathers who have never been closely involved with their children. There is no more intimate relationship between two beings than pregnancy, and a basic psychological preparation for nurturing may also contribute to the potentially catastrophic sense of unfinished business experienced by many women who give up their new-born infants for adoption.

Individuals' response to parenthood is strongly shaped by genetic potentialities, inherited social behaviours (through what Richard Dawkins has labelled 'memes'), and the emotionally-laden memories of childhood. These effects not only alter the content of particular motivational assessments, and so the motivation which emerges in each case, but they also reconstitute the motivational system itself. For example, they induce new skills through that age-old route: learning by teaching others. In this case, although it is the children who are deliberately taught, the act of teaching remoulds the parents' own awareness in such general ways that their whole approach to motivational assessment can be altered.

This biology-led phase-change is of central importance in the whole motivation story, and has profound effects on wider social realities. It is essential for the replication and long term survival of the human race, yet numerous official policies weaken its grip. One example, of many, is the reluctance of politicians (still predominantly male) to provide both parents with entitlement to adequate parental leave. Another is lack of policy to counter the appalling effects of child abuse and child pornography. If the long-term potential of such actions for damaging instinctive parenting skills through subsequent generations was fully recognised, there would be even more pressure to deal with them effectively.

Grandparenthood and generativity
A second major phase change, this time more gradual, takes place later, when the first grandchildren arrive. This may be anytime from the forties onwards, but is increasingly delayed until the late fifties or sixties, as successive generations of younger women develop career ambitions and delay parenthood.

Genes and their cultural equivalent, memes, are strongly at work in grandparenthood too. The result is the emergence of generativity – the concern that individuals' feel for passing on some kind of inheritance to following generations.[14] With this comes a sense of the reciprocation in nurture, as each generation becomes increasingly dependent on its mature offspring. Within the family the role of grandparents, and other relatives of the same generation (to a lesser extent), highlights these concerns and principles.

As with nurture, generativity is essential for the long-term survival and advancement of the species. It helps to put a human face on the long-term cost of greed. Without generativity, there would be little or no conservation or altruism across the genera-

tions, and humanity would slacken in its task of raising new generations to maturity. It is all too easy to see how it could kill itself off by asset-stripping the planet's resources within the span of a very few generations.

Generativity has such a general effect on motivational assessments that it counts as a change in the characteristic settings of individuals' motivational systems. In particular, it produces a marked change in older people's motivation to use their experience in helping younger generations to develop their motivation, and to establish their particular choices in learning and in life.

Family influence on motivation
Against this background we now look at how families can influence the development of motivation of their members, what motivates families to pick up the traces, and their chances of being effective.

Figure 5.2 shows how the family as a collective unit allocates roles and resources (time and money) to developing motivation for both its younger and older members. The effectiveness of family influence depends greatly on these arrangements, which we shall look at more closely in the next chapter. Here we concentrate on two issues: how and to what extent the motivation of family members, of any age, can be influenced; and how the influencers – family members assigned the influencing role – get the skills and motivation to do the work.

Influencing family members: children and young people
The composite box at the bottom centre of Figure 5.2 shows the four main ways in which developmental influence can be exerted on younger family members:

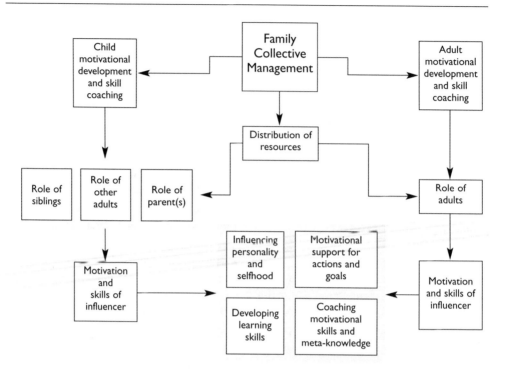

Figure 5.2   Family influence on individual motivational development

• Influencing personality traits and selfhood: At the most fundamental level, parents and other older relatives can aim to influence development of the motivation process indirectly, by trying to control children's emerging personality profiles and the shaping of their self-concept. There are certain orientations and self-concepts which, if inculcated into the young, appear to strengthen motivation, other things being equal. It is widely seen as a key parental responsibility to instil these.

• Coaching high level motivational skills: Parents and others can try to tackle the general effectiveness of children's motivational assessments wherever they are applied. If they see scope for improvement, they can build up the children's high-level skills of motivational assessment, and meta

knowledge about these skills. They can also build on young children's innate tendency to imitate older siblings' skills, where appropriate.

• Developing learning skills and confidence: Parents and others can improve children's learning skills and confidence by involving them in enjoyable projects involving learning, which will encourage them to feel good about learning (promote their learning efficacy) and reduce the amount of time and effort they will subsequently need to put into it (increase their learning efficiency). In this way, successful learning boosts motivation.

• Giving motivational support for particular learning actions and goals: This can be developmental in the sense that particular interventions by parents (and others) can rub off onto the young person's general assessment processes and skills. This is learning by doing and by experience.

Research shows that most of these broad approaches can influence motivation in the short term, for specific things. But whether any of the four is effective in terms of lasting developmental influence remains much debated. In particular, it is not certain that parents have much leverage on the personalities and self-concepts of their children.[15] Any gains produced by skill-based approaches may decay, if good practice is not kept up. We now take a closer look at each of the four approaches.

Shaping the personality – Fierce debates rage about the effectiveness of families in trying to shape children's personalities, whether by altering personal traits, or by creating personality orientations.[16]

Personality traits include a long and varied list of characteristics, including for example: conscientiousness, sympathy, honesty, violence, unpredictability, and meanness. Such traits are general tendencies, supposedly consistently discernible in individuals' behaviour across time and in a range of situations. On the face of it, some obvious personality traits could have motivational consequences.

Research has, for example, shown that conscientiousness as a trait correlates with motivation, other things being equal.[17] Conscientious people who are aware of this as their trait description, who accept it, and who see it as a matter of pride, can predict that they will make strong efforts towards a learning goal. This can help them to feel more capable of obtaining the desired result.

Other potentially useful personality traits could relate directly to characteristic features of motivational assessments themselves, or to the values which people draw into their assessments. These include among others: altruism, hedonism, independence, self-confidence, creativity, futurity/far-sightedness, and fecklessness.

Personality orientations are behavioural response patterns of a more complex kind also, supposedly, discernible in behaviours across the board. They are psychological propensities, which combine in particular ways how individuals think, feel and focus attention. The three orientations most directly relevant to learning motivation are associated mainly with coping behaviour: mastery orientation; normative orientation; and performance orientation.[18]

• Mastery orientation: This 'never give up' response is strongly conducive to motivation and learning success. It is thought to be related to authoritative parenting which encourages children's autonomy and experiment, supports and praises effort, and which accepts any failings in their performance.[19]

• Normative orientation: This is where a person tends to comply with wishes or obligations set down by others.[20] It is often associated with bad feelings because of low autonomy. In choosing and working for goals, people with a normative orientation try to avoid blotting their copy book – and will avoid breaching the relevant norms, rather than face up to positive new challenges. They prefer to minimize the chances of making a mistake (being wrong), rather than take a risk on the chances of victory (being right). They are very prone to fall into learning helplessness, if failure which cannot be ducked or explained away threatens to attract disapproval. This orientation is thought to relate to punitive and rule-bound regimes of parental discipline, and seems to be more evident among girls than boys.

• Performance orientation: This is a specific form of the normative orientation. Instead of fear of moral condemnation, the fear in this case is of disappointing a parent's (and by extension the individual's own) high expectations of learning performance. This is often related to parents constantly expressing high opinions of their children's cleverness, and producing a fear that love will be withdrawn if performance disappoints. Under the performance orientation, fear of falling short of a performance standard becomes more important than the learning goal itself. In educational contexts such people often deliberately handicap themselves, so that the true implications of their ability cannot be clearly drawn. Again, learning persistence is brittle, and risks of dropout are high.

Personality traits and orientations relate to objective behaviour, but they can also usefully be seen as myths or narratives concerning individuals' behaviour patterns. Every family develops such myths, often around a kernel of fact, and attaches them to its various members – "She's like that because she was sent away to boarding school". Individuals may also create or adopt them for themselves, for convenience – "I can't sleep with the window closed because we always slept with it open when I was a kid". Personal narratives are fed by shared half-memories within the family – "Do you remember when...?" – growing in influence through repetition over the years. They

assert perceived behavioural regularities, and are subject to all manner of bias, salience and selectivity in perception.

These narratives threaten to become part of the self-concept, and individuals often try to verify or disprove them by acting out the traits and orientations in real life.[21] The role of the nurturer, on the other hand, is to reinforce or counter the child's own conclusions, by seeking to instil self-descriptions which the parents or others want the child to live up to. It is as if nurturers, by their actions and comments, hold up a mirror to the growing child: "See this good, clever child? Why, its you!" Potentially, almost any self-description can be induced in these ways. Such narratives are not necessarily consistent between themselves, nor are they always consistently maintained over time.

When the narratives are adopted as self-descriptions, they will hopefully include some the child can be proud of. This is where personality enters into motivational development, for it is in the area of approved self-descriptions that self-esteem Brownie points come to be counted. These are gained when an action confirms an important narrative, and lost when it conflicts with it. Parents and others who want to influence motivation by promoting child-approved self-descriptions need to induce them with consistency and determination.

One serious drawback to this, however, is the risk that the child will develop a sense of inauthenticity.[22] A considerable gap can open up between the self-descriptions which nurturers are pressing on the child, or taking for granted in arrangements for education and family life, and the child's own private interpretations. If the parent asserts the description too energetically, the child can grow suspicious of the image, and form a private inner view of the self which is at variance with the official imposed – intro-jected – parental narrative. These gaps can widen and lead to greater fragmentation of the self. According to self-determination theory, if a person is acting out an intro-jected self – created in response to pressure from nurturers – motivation will draw on contingent self-esteem; that is, self-esteem related to fulfilling the expected role in the required character. This will be at the cost of a parallel loss of true self-esteem, because the action contradicts the child's inner view of his or her true self. This loss can be very damaging.

A child who is privately doubtful of a parental view that she is very musical, for example, would feel a degree of lukewarm contingent self-esteem on passing a music exam. But she would also feel a degree of inauthenticity, due to a loss of true self-esteem, because this achievement in parental terms threatens the child's view of her underlying true self. The two effects offset one against the other.

An important question is how far the family context can, in practice, alter and fine-tune children's personality characteristics and orientations. The conventional wisdom is that the family context is immensely influen-tial. In particular, motivational assessments in general would work differently, and would have different content, as a result of family influence. A large part of educational prac-tice and policy seems to rely on this view.

Unfortunately, the research evidence does not provide strong support for it.[23] There are several important factors:

- To the extent that poverty, bad housing and poor health are concentrated in par-ticular social groups, such high levels of stress can be created that parents find the task of shaping personality in particular ways beyond them. The effects are cumula-tive from one generation to another: they are beaten before they start.[24]

- Even if the parents make great efforts, it may simply not be practicable – particu-larly in large families – to control the micro-environment and the experiences of each child to the point of having a clear effect on personality. An important reason for this is children's innate tendency to seek out or make micro-environments to support their basic proclivities.

- It is very likely that adolescents' social life outside the home, at school or in the local community is particularly telling.[25] The bio-logical imperative, developed to drive young people to form new families of their own, is easily strong enough to drown out parental efforts.

- Finally, and most difficult, is the effect of the parental genes. Studies of twins and of adopted children have been extensively undertaken in an effort to gauge the rela-tive importance of genes (nature) and rearing (nurture) in formulating personal-ity. These show the genetic effect to be very strong. For example, the variability of standard personality measures taken on adult twins is affected only to a very small extent by whether those twins have been reared together in the same family context, or apart. If true, any strivings of parents leave very little distinctive mark, over and above the genetic effect, by the time the children are mature adults.

Much more research is needed on these important matters. It would, however, be highly irresponsible, in this field of controversy, to give up all notion that parents can make a difference to personality in defiance of the genes or social determinism. Such a policy might cause a problematic swing to eugenics, or to social and ethnic cleansing. It would also leave educational policy and practice stranded. The most responsible stance, at least for the time being, must surely be to support the family in socially and individually advantageous personality development, both in relation to motivational processes and for other purposes, however hard and controversial that might be. Such a course would not exclude considerable attention also being paid to peer groups and to wider issues of poverty and social exclusion.

Coaching the skills of motivational assessment – Personality is happily not the only means of motivational influence open to parents and families. Motivation involves skills or habits of mental processing which can be conditioned in young people by a range of means: praise, blame, reward, demonstration, support, and various forms of persuasion. This is a very promising approach, not least because there is doubt on the personality-shaping route and, as it happens, the things that parents would do to instil personality are hardly different from what is needed to coach motivational assessment skills. The skills might be shorter-lived compared to personality measures, but the parenting regime would be similar.

Peter is an ebullient boy, with an exceptional natural talent for playing the flute (like his grandfather). That talent is determined by the genes, and encouraged by family tradition, but

Peter still requires good coaching to push his talent to its natural limits. Although he reached intermediate grade level at a fairly young age, with relatively little effort, his parents recognise that he needs coaching to develop his technique beyond that, and that he can only maintain the improvement if he practices regularly. If the coaching stops, his progress marks time.

In much the same vein, children have the capacity to benefit from motivational coaching, within the broad limits that the genes may set.[26] This can be done by experts, but parents and others in the family can acquire the capacity to coach motivation themselves, and will be well placed to do so if the child is living at home.

Peter's twin brother, Paul, is moderately good at most things, but has shown no particular talents. He is much quieter than Peter, and happy to let Peter take the lead most of the time. He is also thoroughly disorganised, yet he can focus and persist – usually over relatively trivial things (in his parents' view) like his collection of matchboxes. Paul has no strong feelings for any particular subjects at school, and spends a lot of time "messing about aimlessly", according to his exasperated father. When he is 14, Paul spends a week in the Peak District on a school-organised trip (while Peter goes off to a music course). Working in small groups, the students learn about setting all kinds of personal, self-selected goals – some fun, some serious – and then work together to achieve those goals. By the end of the week, which he has enjoyed more and more, Paul has learnt some new ways of thinking about things – to the point that he finds it easier to make decisions and he knows how to apply them. He also feels more self-confident. He has discovered a new passion for rock formations and, encouraged by a tutor at the study centre, has decided to find out more about studying Geology. He doesn't feel he has left his old chaotic self behind altogether, but now he does see some point in being more organised, and he is getting better at taking initiative.

Coaching of this kind is becoming more and more practised in the UK by adults and children alike – though generally beyond a formal curriculum. Unlike the contested area of shaping personality, the coaching of motivational skills can prove effective very quickly. As long as the individual sustains the effort, the improvement is maintained. Policies to promote such coaching more widely could be very significant for motivation. If meta-knowledge about motivation (knowledge about motivation itself) is added to the coaching, the improvement is likely to be deeper and longer-lasting.

Learning skills – Basic learning skills and competence (often misleadingly called learning strategies) are the third area where family activity can influence motivation. This is not about the mental process itself, but about how learning skills can be used to benefit it. If improvement in the motivational assessment can boost motivation for particular actions, improvement in learning skills can add a further boost. The effect works by reducing perceived learning cost, which raises net value, and also by improving self-efficacy. These improvements include, among other things: core reading and writing skills; numeracy; deductive and lateral thinking; study skills; information gathering capabilities; listening; reflecting; memorising; record-keeping and more. The combined effect of these on motivation is very significant. Many of these skills are so generally

useful that any depreciation over time is likely to be slow.

Supporting particular learning actions and goals – The fourth and last mode of influencing motivational development is by the simple means of supporting and encouraging young people in specific learning projects or strategies.[27] This may well be done for reasons which are not essentially developmental, but individuals who go through motivational assessments are bound to dwell upon their experience. Suitably guided, they can learn a great deal of value by these means. Figure 5.3 shows particular ways for influencers to gain leverage. As in the case of coaching, the effects of this approach on personal motivational development are not likely to be permanent. The knowledge and skills acquired by usage can be forgotten, or atrophy, if not regularly refreshed by new motivational assessments. Content is important of course, since what is learned by these means need not be always good or advantageous. Poor attitudes and superficial stereotypical thinking can be impressed on the young just as easily as the reverse.

Influencing adults in the family
Figure 5.2 shows that the ways that a family can influence motivational development for adult members are much the same as for younger members. There are a few particular features in this case:

• The general scope for helping older members in the family is less than for young people, but certainly still significant. Clearly if adults are to play the larger role in helping young people, it will help if they themselves have received support of just the same kind within the context of the

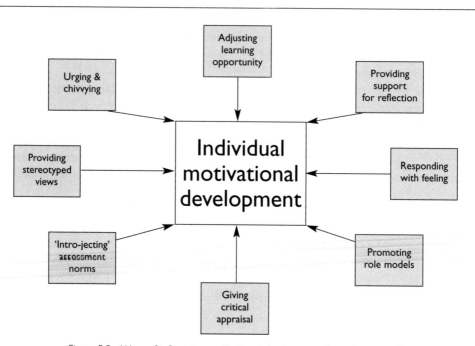

Figure 5.3   Ways of influencing motivational development for actions or goals

family. Policies that always put young people first may have to be reconsidered from this point of view.

- Adults are generally unlikely to be willing to have their personalities influenced and their self-concepts altered so that their motivational processes will correspond to someone else's idea of what is better. Anything they are prepared to do is going to be self-directed and voluntary, as an exercise in autonomy. To make significant progress transformative learning centred on self-realisation is likely to be needed.

- The motivational boost from improved learning skills is not likely to be affected much by age. While mental facility reduces somewhat with advancing years, research evidence strongly suggests that growing experience of learning, and canny self-management, can offset nearly all the deterioration, until the final stage of a long life.[28]

- There is large scope for passing round motivational meta-knowledge and coaching skills among adult members of families, as part of a concerted and consistent effort to motivate the young. If families have no overall agreed approach, individual efforts may confuse, or even cancel each other out.

Having the skill and will to apply influence
Whatever potential a family may have to develop learning motivation, it can only be realised if the family members with influencing roles have the skills and knowledge to do what is needed, and are motivated to carry it out (see the boxes at bottom right and bottom left in Figure 5.2).[29]

Skills – Well-targeted studies are needed, exploring the motivational skills and meta-knowledge required for the kinds of influencing roles which families make possible. This includes the specialised area of parenting skills, but goes well beyond them, to include the defining and managing of roles, and distributing resources to support them, within the family.

Much can be achieved by providing appropriate learning opportunities, inside and outside the family, and by drawing on the resources of other families within local communities and networks. But a good deal can also be done simply by recognising that many families have acquired considerable experience and implicit knowledge in this area which can be drawn out, consolidated, applied and passed on with profit.

Motivation – A nurturer's energy and persistence in bringing up children is produced by a motivational process much like that explored in Chapters 3 and 4, involving net value (of nurturing, in this case) and the probability of success. The nature of the motivational process will reflect in its detail the standing and situation of the influencer – as parent, sibling, or other family member.

The role of parents' own motivation for developing their children's motivational and learning skills cannot be overestimated. It is arguable whether anyone else has anything like the same chance of influence – whether for good or ill. The net value can be a serious challenge to parents in the family, because it raises the whole purpose of good parenting. Is it investment for old age? Is it for keeping a social reputation, or obeying a moral or religious creed? Is it simply justified on the principle of a stitch in time saves nine? The

trade-offs here are very closely tied up with nurturers' own goal hierarchies, and negotiations among the various people involved. Parents can gain a great deal from parenting courses which clarify aspects of value, in appropriate terms.

The probability angle for parents has two aspects:

• If the parent comes to believe that his or her influence has no lasting effect on children's motivational processes, there will be a reluctance to enter the fray. This is a weak means-ends belief.

• Some parents come to believe that their children will resist and defeat any efforts or campaigns that their parents attempt. This is an issue of self-efficacy.

Poor parenting skills and very difficult domestic circumstances can easily turn every parental initiative into an emotive battle over the child's autonomy. Despite specialisation of nurturing roles within the family, parents – singly or together – often fail to cope, and become helpless; or they just go through the motions, disclaiming responsibility for developing the child. Vicious circles are commonplace, particularly if the parents themselves received little experience of good parenting as children. Where inexperienced parents show signs of not coping, grandparents and other relatives can provide crucial support within the family, along with parenting courses in the community.

Notes and references (Numbers refer to publications listed in the Reference section)

1   See Smith & Spurling 223 for a more extensive treatment of family motivation.

2   See Smith & Spurling 222, Abrams & Hogg 1; also 34, 70, 140, 141, 154 & 171.

3   For background on the workplace see 8, 95, 115, 116 & 139. See Smith & Spurling 221.

4   See Harter 125 for a detailed study of key developmental processes in children.

[5] See Skinner 123; also 112, 151.

[6] See Skinner 212; also 87.

[7] See 73, 150.

[8] See Adams 3.

[9] See 70.

[10] See 69, 142, 197.

[11] This is closely associated with development in moral thinking. See Read 199.

[12] See Alwin 6.

[13] See 165.

[14] See 30, 128.

[15] See Harris 123, 124.

[16] See Caspi 39.

[17] See 46.

[18] See Stipek 229 for a good discussion of orientations; also 24, 74, 75.

[19] See 179.

[20] See 133, 134.

[21] See 144.

[22] See 202.

[23] See Harris 123 for an important review; also Caspi 39.

[24] See Halsey 120.

[25] See Harris 124 for a good discussion of this.

[26] See 222 for discussion of a transformative learning approach based on coaching.

[27] Most of these factors are examined systematically in Bandura 9.

[28] See 65, 128, 167, 232.

[29] See 28, 111, 165, 211.

Chapter 6:
The family's wider influence on motivation

Introduction

In the interests of motivation, family members can seek to influence each other for reasons beyond development. This might be in their own interest; for their own convenience; for their individual altruism; or out of some family objective, where the driver is group motivation. The influence is not restricted to that between nurturer and child, but may be between two individuals of different generations – grandparent and grandchild is very common – and between partners in any generation. On this wider front there are a number of issues about the ways that families can organise themselves to make the most of motivational influence.

Influencing motivation and motivational development

Before engaging with these organisational themes, we look briefly at how family members of any generation influence each other's motivation for learning projects and strategies.[1]

Figure 5.3, page 61, set out the main ways that an influencer can seek in directing an individual's motivation, if the purpose is developmental through experiential learning. This is now extended in Figure 6.1 on page 66. It includes a number of additional levers which, while not particularly developmental, can be effective in the wider context. The additional elements are shown with shaded background.

All these kinds of influence can be found in every family from time to time, sometimes with a positive influence on motivation, and sometimes not. For example:

- Incentives: "Go on! If you finish your homework in time, you can come to the skate centre with us."[2]

- Opportunity: "Gran's invited you to stay with her while you're revising for your exams, if you'd like to. It's quieter there."

- Support: "Give us a shout if you get stuck – I'll give you a hand. And have a look at that web site I was talking about."

- Reflection: "Well, you could make a note of five things you've learnt from doing GCSE, which might make working for A levels go better."[3]

- Response with feeling: "What ever's that meant to be! Call that a cake? Just a waste of good food, if you ask me."

- Role model: "I did the same course last year – it's OK once you've started. If I can manage it, you can!"

- Information: "You can learn computing down at the drop-in centre in town, for free. Go in any time you want, and work at your own speed."[4]

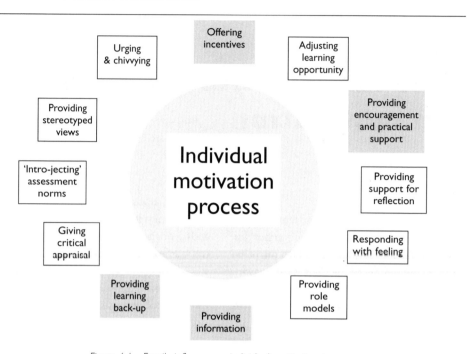

Figure 6.1   Family influence on individual motivation process

- Learning stocks available: "I've got all my books from last year, if you want to use them. And my notes too, if they'd be helpful. Cherry Halsey's book is well worth reading."[5]

- Critical appraisal: "I've had a look at those units on numeracy. I reckon they're very user-friendly – just the thing for brushing up on long division, percentages and things."

- Assessment norms: "Book reading's never done this family no good. What's the point? No job is no job."

- Stereotyped view: "Classical music's got no beat."

- Urging: "Go on, have a go! What've you got to lose? I warn you, I'm going to keep on about this, because it's important – not just for you but for all of us."

There is no shortage of ways to apply influence, and overall the potential for motivational influence within the family is very strong. It may not always be for the good, of course.[6] Family breakdown, or low family efficacy in applying these influences, can have very severe effects on individual members' levels of motivation. As poor learning experiences are shared, levels of motivation can plummet for the individual concerned and for others in the family, casting a long shadow on subsequent learning.

There are some particularly important points in the family context:

- Children are particularly good at instinctive copying, so role models can be very effective.[7] Adults too are very sensitive to role modelling, picking up implicit values and information to test self-efficacy. The values and information need to be good, if the motivational influence is to be beneficial.

- Incentives might be expected to be effective, if they increase extrinsic value or remove extrinsic harm. But experience shows that people will often resist the manipulation which incentives involve, in order to protect their self-esteem.[8] Or they see an offered incentive as a bribe, signifying some level of desperation in the offerer. As a result they may up the ante, in the hope of raising the value of the bribe. Even infants know how to do this.

- The stock of knowledge available and accessible as a contingent provision in the family can be very reassuring. This is part of social capital (see below).

- Tactful chivvying can tip the balance. It sets up a new bit of net value, which is the effect of relief when the victim gives in and the chivvying stops. Fear of jeopardizing affection also counts very highly.

- If people are looking for quick closure on their motivational assessments,[9] or have poor assessment skills or opportunities, the casual stereotypical evaluations and attitudes of family members can be picked up and adopted wholesale. Parents and other nurturers need to be alert to this.

Organisation for motivational influencing in the family

But how does a family organise itself, both to raise motivation for specific actions and to develop individual members' motivational skills and processes? Important issues of social capital, role assignment, helping, and group identity all need to be considered, and there are questions about resources and external factors influencing the family from outside, with a marked knock-on effect on the family's internal motivating activity.

Social capital for learning within the family

Social capital can be defined as a generally-supportive environment within a particular society or social group.[10] It provides a resource for group members, which they can rely on for contingencies, over and above any specific relationships of help, support or exchange which may exist between them. Social capital is built by social interactions which establish mutual recognition, or – going further – create reciprocity in obligation. The psychology of this is well understood by anybody who has ever felt able to borrow a ladder from their neighbour, or who is happy to feed the neighbours' cat when they are away on holiday. If a person can be asked, social capital exists.

Social capital can exist for families as well as for wider social groupings. Like all social capital, it can have specific forms. In the case of learning, the more family members support each other on learning motivation, the more social capital for learning they build up within the family, for family members to enjoy. The interaction amounts to a buzz-factor within the group.

The contingency stocks of resources in social capital are a form of insurance for the individuals who can draw upon them. They provide flows of support services, should the need arise, over and above those that members of the relevant group would normally receive (see Figure 6.2). Even if these services are never actually used, the fact that they are available has option value, like having a spare wheel in the back of the family car. In the learning field, this option value comes from knowing that help is readily available. It can greatly strengthen individuals' motivation by reducing personal risk.

Whether or not individuals value the possibility of receiving support depends on a number of factors:

- location: where they are in relation to the various resource stocks;
- supply routes: whether there are the means to supply the services to them;
- group saliency: whether the individuals have developed the group-saliency that enables them to perceive a potential resource;
- eligibility: what understandings there are about eligibility for support;[11]
- self-esteem: whether individuals feel able to ask for, accept or offer help, without threatening self-esteem.[12]

Rebellious teenagers trying to establish a sense of autonomy, for example, may be blind to potential support inside the family, until they recognise family saliency in their own terms. Even then, they need to know how to ask for help without threatening their sense of self-esteem; and other family members need to know how to offer it, so that the chance of rebuttal does not threaten their self-esteem.

Given frequent, supportive contact between members, the family has endless opportunities for building up stocks of social capital for learning goals and strategies. The larger the stocks, the more services there are to flow, but the flow to each individual will depend on the quality of the affection and involvement within the family. The closer the family in terms of group identity, degrees of altruism, proximity (physical and emotional), family roles, and practical living arrangements, the more easily support can flow to each family member. The greater the distances between the members – reflected in individual living arrangements, jealousies and resentments, and maintained by destructive narratives – the more effort is needed to build social capital.[13]

In the area of social capital, affection can overcome the disadvantages of physical separation to some extent, just as lack of affection undermines the advantages of physical proximity. The mobile telephone, and the ubiquitous non-urgent conversations that so annoy other people, are a case in point. They may sound superficial or meaningless to non-participants, but the

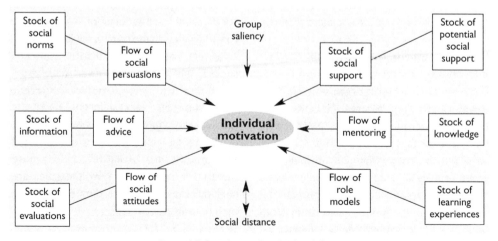

Figure 6.2 Social capital and related flows

sheer act of communicating builds and maintains social capital between the callers. The message that matters is not so much the articulated one, "The train gets in at 6.30", it is the implied one, "I'm on my way home, and I'm looking forward to seeing you". That is why the intermittent sound of mobile telephones is so distressing for people clearing up after a railway accident: it is a reminder of disrupted relationships.

Conversely, however tightly packed a family may be in the home, and however much the individuals might, in theory, have to contribute, if any member is not prepared to share what he or she has, everybody loses out. In these terms, dysfunctional families represent an appalling waste of potential for learning motivation.

Social capital within the family is built not only by specific interactions and activities, but also by its direct promotion among family members. Deliberately building a family's social capital amounts to managing good, warm contact between the individuals, and between the generations. Such management enables some family units to contribute to, and draw on, a fund of social capital in the wider family despite being separated by whole continents, while lack of it ensures that other families remain impoverished even though they live in the same house. Much more research is needed into how social capital for learning in the family works, and how it can best be fostered.

Development of specialised motivational roles within the family
The warm glow of social capital for learning is important, but there is much more for a family to do in organising its influence of motivation to learn. There is also the question of how families set themselves up to carry out the main ongoing and specific acts of motivational support and coaching.[14]

This is first and foremost a matter of roles. In many families, for example, one or other parent is routinely absent from most of the daily nurturing role, including day-by-day learning support, but will dip in occasionally for particular purposes. In some families, both parents are absent for most of the time, and grandparents or other relatives may have a large role. Older children may be given particular roles regarding younger siblings.[15] The different patterns of roles are numerous, and very significant for learning motivation. A key question for any family is therefore how the responsibilities for nurture and informal coaching in the learning domain are distributed. Are they left to happen, or not, haphazardly? Are the role patterns clear, stable and effective? And how are they managed in the light of their effectiveness?

The role patterns are determined in a seemingly endless number of different ways. Some may be negotiated and determined by agreement; some are imposed according to power relations between individuals; some are adopted as cultural norms, ranging from hierarchical collectivism to egalitarian individualism;[16] some are expressions of the family group identity. Factors of culture and of identity tend to go together. The collectivist family is very different from the individualist family, and leaves a characteristic imprint on family members' self-concepts and motivational processes. Much more research is needed on how the roles are clarified, and what effect they have on the family's motivational task.

Where roles are not predetermined, there

is scope for some negotiation and choice. Self-maintenance theory has shed light on how such negotiation might work, both to condition family members' motivation for their own learning, but also to produce a distribution of motivational roles among adult members of the family.[17] According to this theory, each individual is motivated to maintain a high level of self-esteem relating to personal achievement, compared to the others. A learning example shows how this works.

Jas has exceptional mathematical ability. Her younger sister, Abbi, is also good but not quite in the same league. Even if Abbi were to focus on maths – as her relative ability compared to her classmates might suggest – she is nonetheless likely to feel put out and inadequate by comparison with her brilliant sister. So, to maintain favourable self-evaluation, Abbi underplays her mathematical aptitude, and looks for something else to specialise in, to avoid invidious comparisons of mathematical performance. She develops a particular keenness for athletics instead – an interest they also share. At the same time, Abbi may gain some personal benefit from her sister's success: her self-esteem may be boosted through her relationship to somebody held in esteem beyond the home. Also, because she and Jas are very close, she quite simply feels altruistic pleasure for her sister's achievements – as Jas does for Abbi's successes on the track.

In the example, Jas has high self-esteem from her own mathematical performance; but at the same time she would be chary of outshining Abbi in her chosen area of athletics, even though the elder sister might well be able to compete strongly in that field if she put her mind to it. So she backs off from the athletics, and gets real pleasure from

supporting Abbi and celebrating her success in that field.

Left to themselves, therefore, each of these sisters is likely to specialise, favouring areas they are particularly good at and where the other is perhaps a little less so. Apart from the comparison of abilities, an activity is more likely to become a speciality if it is valued highly by the chooser, and if the family has given the chooser some authority or power in that area. In effect, each sister will enhance her self-esteem and other items of net value by side-stepping the reputational competition between them. The basking in reflected glory, or empathy effects, will pull against the tendency to specialise, but commonly will not be strong enough to stop it.[18]

This specialising tendency is commonly seen among siblings, but the theory works for other family pairings too, notably between partners or spouses. The problem with the specialising/avoiding tendency, when played out over time, is that it can box able people into performance dead ends, and prevent them from learning in areas where they have much to contribute. If, for example, people choose partners who have similar interests and talents, and one has to give way to the other, a great deal of potential can be lost. Colleges and universities are familiar with the fact that many mature women who return to learning after child-rearing subsequently experience serious marital problems. A major contributor is the way that the woman's new learning challenges a long-standing balance of specialisation between the partners.

There are two ways that unwelcome competition within the family can be disarmed. In the first, the two individuals pursue the activity jointly, but with some degree of spe-cialisation within the activity (musical siblings learn different instruments, for example). In the second, they each maintain the same activity, but normally avoid doing it together, except for fun. Psychologists call this 'distancing'. Specialisation of this kind comes to form part of the self-concept, both for the individuals concerned and for family identity.

These dynamics are important for learning motivation inside the family, but they are often also at work in shaping motivational influencing roles within the family. Cultural stereotyping plays a role, too. Commonly, for example, fathers still tend to specialise in athletic pursuits, leaving mothers to do the school run and associated nurturing chores.[19] So mothers end up supporting the children on most aspects of school motivation, possibly neglecting her own learning needs into the bargain; while fathers put time into promoting athletic prowess, particularly for their sons.

In sum, not only does the influencing activity of the family depend on social capital in the home, it also depends greatly on the cultural norms which organise the family, and on the psychological processes operating between pairs of family members. The resulting arrangements may be deeply unsatisfactory for some of the individuals involved, needing a great deal of help to sort them out.

Altruism and helping
Another important factor is the degree of altruism and specific helping which is available in the family.[20] This is important for the specific influence on motivation for actions and goals. It is also highly relevant for social capital.

Groups are evolution's answer to individu-als' need to survive and prosper in a hostile environment. Helping, and particularly recip-rocal helping, is a key aspect of group behaviour. Reciprocity (graphically expressed among primates by the practice of mutual grooming) is very important also in humans, across all cultures. It makes for more success in positive actions, offers collective security in defence, and ensures that people do not become over-dependent on help from strangers.

A person might offer motivational support for a relative's learning for a number of rea-sons. It may be in the expectation of some reciprocation later; or because it promises some gain in reputation and self-esteem, by association; or because it offers the possibil-ity of intrinsic value by easing the relative's discomfiture; or by expressing sympathy, guilt or moral obligation towards the other. These various reactions are not necessarily exclusive of each another.

Helping behaviour has been thoroughly researched. A great deal of social sensitivity and skill must be involved, if helping is to be successful. A would-be benefactor has to size up the opportunity to help carefully, taking into consideration the likely reaction of the person to be helped. Will he resent the offer of help? Will her independence be undermined? At the same time the person needing help has to know how to go about seeking it, and what the dangers are, both in terms of personal self-perceptions and in terms of how the attitudes of the helpers are likely to be affected.

The amount of helping that takes place in a family, over motivational issues as well as other things, depends therefore on the learning about helping which individual family members have already accumulated. Much of this knowledge will have been acquired informally during childhood.[21] If helping is to happen, people must know how to offer it, and how to receive it. Research indicates that genetic inheritance may play a part in the emergence of helping behaviours within the family, but that still leaves room for important skills to be consciously developed and applied. At every turn there are self-esteem barriers – masquerading as stubbornness, or independence, or stand-offishness – hiding a fear of help being spurned. Negotiating and procedural skills are needed to overcome these difficulties, forming an important part of what has been labelled Emotional Intelligence.[22]

Family identity
Yet for all this talk of social capital, roles, mutual back scratching and helping within the family, an essence of family has still to be captured. The family has the potential to be more than a cockpit for assembling and trading off individual members' mutual and warring interests.[23] It can be an entity in its own right, with its own family identity. Sometimes the identity is obvious; but in many cases it is implicit, and it takes a family crisis or tragedy, and a change of saliency, to discover its fundamental importance.

Within the total compass of an individual's self-concept, social psychologists have distinguished a set of partially-separated self-concepts which cluster around the true self, each with its own distinctive motivational processes.[24] Inconsistency in motivation arises when saliency is switched from one such self to another. These selves consist of individual identities and group identities.[25] When an individual identity is

salient, an 'I' motivation comes to the fore. When a group identity is salient, the person identifies himself or herself as a member of a particular group of people, and this brings that person's relevant 'we' motivation into the spotlight.

Individuals can shift saliency between these two categories quite readily. This switching is rather like the effect of counterchange patterns found in Islamic, Greek and Mexican art, where figure and ground can both be seen as the positive or the negative part of the pattern. When one functions as the figure, the other has to function as the field that throws it into prominence. In a similar way, people switch back and forth between their 'I' and 'we' identities according to what suits their situation.

Group identities referring to non-family groups will be explored in the next chapter. Here the key point is that family identity is an important example of group identity, except for some people living alone or true orphans. When family identity is salient for family members, they are thinking of themselves as part of the family collective, not as individuals within the family. Many people may have more than one such family identity, to account for possible cultural differences between a home family and their extended family, or when there are broken families and step-relationships to consider.

Individuals inside families can be influenced and helped in their I-motivations to undertake learning; but they can also be influenced towards learning by developing an appropriate family identity. The family can foster such an identity, and the narratives which go with it, and develop ways to keep it salient. The aim in doing so is to encourage more effective joint action, and a definite benefit is a reduction of bickering. If the family narratives regarding learning are positive, and if the individual identifies strongly with the family, the individualistic I-motivation is replaced by an even more powerful we-motivation.[26] This works both ways: a family that generally derides learning, as a group, will hinder the learning of its members as long as they individually identify with the negative family narrative.

Family identity can, of course, do more than alter the learning motivation of family members. It can also become a powerful driver for individuals to influence their relatives in their learning motivation, and their motivational knowledge and skill. This requires a strong element in the family narrative to the effect that, "In our family, we encourage each other to have a go at learning", or "In our family, older brothers and sisters are expected to encourage the younger ones". In a similar way, an appropriate family identity can provide a strong framework for social capital amongst family members. As they grow up, young people may well take all this for granted, until they see the cost in families without such support.

Identity groups such as families are more than coalitions of convenience. They quickly develop group stereotypes, both for the particular group concerned (the in-group) and for other groups not included (out-groups).[27] The stereotype is an average member, with typical behaviours, views, self-concepts and – important here – typical motivational processes and assumptions. As a group species, humans have very strong awareness of stereotypes, and rapidly develop unanimity concerning them. They converge on the group stereotype, the

individuals tending to conform to it in behaviour and in psychological processes. The convergence applies to motivational assessment, just as it does to other things.

Common ceremonial practices, symbols, narratives and joint reflection on experience have a role in confirming shared identity within the in-group. These all help to build the stereotype and to mould its particular set of coherent motivations. The practices and narratives become badges and icons, which members assemble to verify their feelings of identity.

All this applies to families, as it does to social groups out in society. Suitably set up, it provides a rich vein of motivation based on group identity. But it comes with a price tag. The factors that draw group members together also create an exaggerated view of the gap between the in-group stereotype and the stereotypes of out-groups. On the back of that, members tend to discriminate in favour of the in-group, and to detract from the reputation of the out-groups. These are the natural, divisive tendencies underpinning social tensions across the globe. Motivation may therefore be strengthened within the family, at the risk of damage to social capital and particular relations between the family and other groups, including other families.

Another difficulty with developing strong 'we' motivation in the family is that a time may come when individual members feel they must leave the family, or at any rate free themselves from a family view which they feel constrains them unreasonably. Giving saliency to individual identity and pushing family identity into the background – for the time being at least – can be difficult.[28] Good family role modelling will help to show that this is a normal developmental process, for individuals at any age, and enable the individual to share thoughts and feelings and explore possible solutions. This is where old family friends can play an important role. If not, and especially if there is too heavy an emphasis on family unity, the individual may feel torn by guilt and heart-searching. Having more than one relevant family identity in play may also cause contradiction and vacillation between the rival we-motivations. This can be a major practical impediment for learning, not least for people whose social and family selves are in flux or turmoil.

Switching in and out of family identity is not restricted to individuals: any family, or sections of it, may share a saliency switch. If this happens, relatives can at one moment see their family as a loose-knit group of individuals, where negotiation is needed to establish a balance of individual interests; and at another moment as an integrated team, with a common identity and joint purpose, and with roles determined within the group according to the common interest. The switching possibility leaves a deep ambiguity, around which the joy and pain of family life revolves.

All in all, the probability is that the benefits from using family identity to bolster motivation for family learning will hugely outweigh the disadvantages. Much more should be done to develop and explore this approach. But great care needs be taken to see that the family's group narrative recognises the need for individual members not to be stifled within an oppressive family structure. The give-and-take of affection must be built in.

Where family identity is engaged in this way the family has the potential to become a Learning Organisation – that is, an organisation where the members, individually and together, all actively pursue learning as a high-level life goal.[29] If that goal is expressed as a lifelong learning goal, the family will function as a Lifelong Learning Organisation.

This model may well not appeal to members of secure, individualistic families. But it has been well tried over the centuries, notably in migration by Jewish families and by families from the Indian subcontinent. It has enabled families escaping racial, religious or political persecution to establish themselves in totally foreign environments.

At the beginning of the 21st century, large numbers of UK-based families face urgent problems which, while not being immediately life-threatening, are problems of family survival. They generally reflect industrial responses to global change, such as those in farming and the production of coal and steel, and the implications of rapid global travel and transportation, such as the outbreak of foot and mouth disease in 2001. The effects of globalization can be brutal, and the challenge of adapting to a radically new life pattern can suddenly rear up in the wake of redundancy, devastation and social exclusion.

Resources and external factors
A sharing of family life is very much a sharing of resources and, as Figure 6.3 shows, a family's resources are very largely determined by its economic and social ties with the outside world. Some families have every chance in the world, others are impoverished to such a degree that the very idea of organising in support of learning is a bad joke. We have both kinds in the UK.

Figure 6.3 shows how the learning motivations of family members reflect the resources of time and money available to the family as a group, and also the flexibility for passing those resources around within that group. Time is limited, and adults have to commit large slices of it to earning money and to basic domestic activities such as eating, sleeping, and maintaining a healthy home. Time for discretionary activity will be at a premium. Money also has to be set aside for essential expenditures, leaving only a margin for possible discretionary use. It can be used to ease time constraints – buying a microwave oven to save time in preparing meals, for example – just as working longer can ease money constraints. Any proposed use of time and/or money for learning will tend to mean going without the alternative that has to be sacrificed. Chapter 1 showed how that sacrifice plays a key role in motivational assessment.

This then is where the external world principally impinges on the motivation of the family and its individual members. Income reflects earnings from employment, and from the state via welfare payments and taxation. Employment impacts on available time. Take away the basic necessities of living, and the family is left with a discretionary margin of time and money for learning and consumption. These are the essential constraints which set up the need for sacrifices to be made in choices between learning action and goals on one hand, and anything else. The effects on learning motivation and, by extension, on the promotion of learning motivation within the family are profound. For example:

• If employment earnings dry up, money budgets tighten. Learning time may then come under pressure, because more work is needed to sustain the family, and

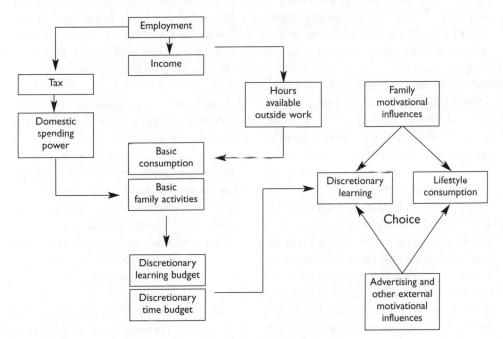

Figure 6.3 Flows of family resources

because labour saving expenditures are squeezed. Learning motivation shrinks because the probability of success goes down, and net value is diminished. There are similar effects if redistributive tax and welfare policies move against the family budget.

• If employment hours have to lengthen, money budgets may benefit from higher earnings, but the time squeeze will increase the family's problems of finding the time for learning and for the support of learning. All this will have an impact, both on learning motivation, and on the energy which parents and others can put into learning support.

• If the market economy is successful in promoting the value the family gives to expenditures which rival learning, then the resources spent on those expenditures will squeeze out motivation for learning and for learning support in the family. This can work through vigorous advertising of the value of products, or through promoting products as a symbol of identity among people of a given age or social group.

Unlike standard economic assumptions, budgets and motivation interrelate, and are not in practice independent of each other. What is more, the motivational effects of changes in the available family budgets will also be related to the success the family has in creating a common pot for family resources; in distributing the resources from it to family members; and in determining how far expenditure from the pot is a family responsibility, or an individual delegation. Misery, for sure, will not necessarily be shared equally. Parents often ignore their own learning needs in favour of their children's immediate needs – a policy which can rob the children of vital role models of learning,

and of more effective support through enhanced stocks of knowledge and valuable social capital within the family. Reaching unanimity among family members on responding to these may stretch family loyalties and internal negotiating skills, and reduce family efficacy all round. This is where a strong family identity as a Learning Organisation can pay very good dividends.

Three other external factors are particularly important:

• The family, as well as the individuals in it, are targets of commercial promotion and advertising. Once the question of available resources is settled, the pull and push of huge commercial expenditures on the advocacy of consumption will have a further serious and significant effect on learning motivation. This is a battle where commercial interests sweep all before them. Learning providers do not commit anything like comparable resources to generic promotion and to outreach. Predominantly, learners go to the learning providers – not the other way round.

• Government has considerable power to influence the family in its capacity as a builder of learning motivation. Figure 6.3 shows that much can be done in a rather general and unfocussed way, through tax and welfare payments. Undoubtedly government could do a great deal more if it made more specific funded interventions to help families organise developmental support roles for learning, and if it advertised consistently to families.

• Lastly, each family which organises itself effectively to promote learning motivation can act as a link in a far wider network of families, working together through community. This creates wider inter-family social capital which can support individual families in their internal efforts and activities. To find ways of fostering this wider social capital is a very important part of developing a Learning Society. Chapter 7 will explore this further. There is, however, the possibility that social capital may work in reverse.

Finally, if external forces apply widely, across whole sets of families, and across whole geographical and employment areas, to damage family learning, the strains within families will be amplified on a wider social canvas.

Notes and references (Numbers refer to publications listed in the Reference section)

[1] Most of these are discussed in Bandura 9.

[2] Incentives can be negative as well as positive. They can cause rejection through injured self-esteem. See 62 for a review.

[3] See Schon 114 for discussion of reflection in a professional context.

[4] See 48.

[5] See 120, and it is.

[6] The question of the moral worth of the objects of motivation is a major theme, not fully explored in this book. See Smith & Spurling 220 for discussion of the minimum moral basis of a lifelong learning culture.

[7] See Harter 125 and Bandura 9.

[8] See Note 2 above.

[9] See Kruglanski in 160.

[10] Social capital is not easy to define. See Halsey 120, and Schuller 208, 209.

[11] Eligibility should be given a fairly broad meaning.

[12] See 210 for self-esteem and helping.

[13] The link between distance and social networks is explored in 63.

[14] The literature on social movements has some relevance to these issues, but at one remove. See 34, 154 & 156.

[15] See 73.

[16] For an excellent review see Triandis 233.

[17] See 16, 191.

[18] It is not clear whether this specialisation process is confined to individualistic cultures, or transcends cultural boundaries.

[19] See 165.

[20] See 210 for a comprehensive account.

[21] See 73.

[22] The popular idea of Emotional Intelligence is due to Goleman 103. See Mayer 169 for an academic examination of the concept.

[23] The classic statement of the trading-off is Buchanan 33 and Olson 181.

[24] See Ryan & Deci 202.

[25] See Abrams & Hogg 1, and Hogg & Abrams 140, 141

[26] The narrative aspect is developed in 148.

[27] See 31 and 16.

[28] See Parr 185 for useful case studies.

[29] Good accounts of what a Learning Organisation feels like are in 41 and 66.

Chapter 7:
Other influential environments

Introduction

This chapter looks in turn at each of the three remaining environments: institutions for learning; communities; and the workplace. It shows how all these environments influence the individual's motivation, and motivational development. It also highlights how the environments overlap, so that the effect of any one of them is dependent on all the others. If motivational policy and practice are to be effective, they need to recognise the wider cat's cradle of forces influencing motivation.

Learning institutions

A host of interests surrounds the developing of learning motivation in institutions. For the most part these are places supplying learning, but they also include learning web sites and other networked organisations. Typical institutions – schools, colleges and universities – are all established for the purposes of learning; in the case of schools this includes controlling and directing (schooling) children's natural instincts and energies. The policies and practices of each institution reflect the intentions of their funders, founders or shareholders, as interpreted by a governing board and the various professionals working in and with the institution. These routinely include teachers, lecturers, managers, health professionals, religious leaders and social workers on a professional basis; and individuals, often including students' relatives, on a voluntary basis. These people deliver learning and mentoring in a number of ways, ranging from formal teaching to extra-curricular activities. In addition to direct and specific influence, the general life of the institution is influential through the example it sets across a broad area, including the way non-professional staff, such as dinner ladies and ground staff, are treated.

To be effective, learning institutions and their professionals need to help learners to develop a strong platform for their individual learning motivation. This means helping students to develop:

- motivation for particular learning projects, and particular learning goals at strategy level; and
- good motivational processing skills, meta-knowledge about motivation, and relevant learning skills.

Figure 7.1 shows the intricate way that motivational influences bear on the learner in a learning institution.

Teachers

At the centre of motivational influence in Figure 7.1 lies teachers' motivation for their teaching role. Just as for parents, the motivation of teachers (and other professionals) as effective influencers depends on their assessment of net value and probability.

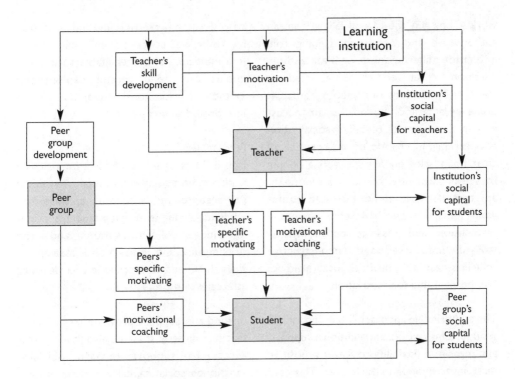

Figure 7.1 The cat's cradle of influence

Their self-efficacy as motivators is enhanced by:
- developing the necessary meta-knowledge of student motivation for the relevant age group, and skills in general motivational coaching and targeted influencing;
- the institution actively supporting and enabling teachers' efforts in spreading meta-knowledge of motivation; coaching students in motivational assessment, by guiding personality development; developing assessment and learning skills; and specific motivating of learning tasks and strategies.

Their net value depends on status and reward, and includes both intrinsic and extrinsic elements. The loss of self-esteem inherent in low pay and being treated as sub-professional technicians is very important. Institutions' efforts in these areas not only

benefit the students, but they also develop motivational social capital among the staff – long-recognised as an essential ingredient in educational effectiveness. This becomes part of a wider social capital from which students can also benefit.

If teachers are to teach well, they have to sustain their motivation – just as parents need optimism to keep at the nurturing task. Both groups are liable to collapse into coping behaviour and helplessness if conditions are poor, if the students are fractious and their behaviour overtaxing, and if necessary support is not forthcoming from the principal, the governors and – in state schools – local and national government.[1]

Teachers, like parents, have to exercise power and authority in their motivational work. They run the risk of falling from an authoritative and consistent guiding role into chaotic libertarianism, or bleak authoritarianism.[2] Wherever a child's unbridled will meets the intentions of society, whether at home or at school, boundaries are necessary in the interests of safety, socialisation and learning. In chaotic conditions, lack of clear boundaries encourages young people to strive constantly for adult attention, at any cost. But rigid authoritarianism pushes young people either towards a normative orientation and loss of autonomy; or towards unfocussed and unconstructive rebelliousness, as a habitual social attitude. Neither is useful for motivation.

The authoritative approach lies in the middle ground, using reason, unconditional support, and measured flexibility to foster a positive mastery orientation in the learner. This goes with teachers giving up the knowledge transmission model – what Paulo Freire calls the banking model – in favour of a facilitative approach.[3] This is a major challenge for staff in localities where children arrive at school with an antisocial, non-cooperative attitude, developed in an area which may lack the basic components of community life, and from homes which are little more than emotional battlefields.

When the influence of teachers and parents align on common bases they reinforce each other, providing clear boundaries and developmental paths.[4] Inconsistency between them causes difficulties, in terms of mixed signals. An important aspect of socialisation is learning to negotiate differences of expectation in different areas of society. But profound differences between parents and teachers can seriously disrupt other learning. To be useful for motivation, planned co-ordination between home and institution has to be well conceived and implemented. In a multicultural and equitable society the implications need careful exploration.[5] Without it, institutional assumptions can be interpreted as arrogance.

Peer groups
Figure 7.1 is based on an ideal for teaching staff: suitably equipped and supported; doing its best to motivate and enthuse the students; aiming to develop students' meta-knowledge of motivation, and the orientations and motivational assessment skills they need to succeed in their learning strategies and projects.

Beyond the support provided by individual teachers directly, students also have indirect access to support through officially-sanctioned social capital within the institution, through mentors, for instance. In addition, they have their peers – a very significant factor indeed. The role of peer groups is shown on the left hand side of Figure 7.1.

Peers pass among themselves a kind of motivational folk-knowledge based on myths, assessment skills and/or bad habits which they have picked up at home and elsewhere.[6] They can help to motivate each other directly regarding particular learning projects and strategies. Peer influence also works generally through the alternative social capital which peers provide within the institution. Neither direct influence nor the less direct support of peer-group social capital is necessarily supportive in the way that the institution might like.

Research evidence bears out the strong influence of peer groups on young people's learning motivation. Their social groupings within education often turn over rapidly, as like seeks out like, and as they try out on each other various self-concepts and group identities. Sometimes the groups will reflect more permanent groupings, in a local or residential community. When young peer-group identity becomes salient, very strong group motivation attaches to it, much as group identity can do within families.

The support offered by such peer groups is especially important for those individuals who value self-concepts which are anti-institutional, in terms of rejecting institutional goals, sometimes to the point of failing in learning, or being notorious in opposing authority. Other individuals, by contrast, might also form small groups, motivating each other to do well in their studies through co-operation, friendly rivalry and their own bit of social capital.[7] This shift to group study is an established trend in higher education. Peer group influence is also important in developing altruism, social sensitivity, and emotional intelligence. It can also sharpen entity beliefs such as, "I'm not very bright", "I'm clever but lazy", "I'm too fat". In further and higher education, peer group influence is also exerted at institutional level through the increasing use of peer-group tutoring and assessment, and through the activity of student unions.

The institution has some control on these influences through the way it structures groups of students, and the efforts it makes to influence student culture towards mutual support and altruistic activity – by encouraging group learning rather than individualistic, competitive learning, for example. Institutional policies on admissions, class formation, streaming/setting, and age-banding all have an impact.

Institutional ethos
But there is more to it than this. The general ethos of the institution is also hugely important.[8] An ethos is the distinctive character, spirit and attitudes of a culture. It is expressed though narratives which depict an ideal style, in this case for the organisation's activities – "This is the way we do things around here". This style will contain elements of procedure, power and ideology or value. In many ways it functions like a personality orientation, writ large. Whereas social capital can be seen as a helping hand in reserve, ethos is a form of social conditioning that seeps into every crack and pore of the organisation. Whatever staff do directly to inculcate motivational skills, and to motivate students to particular achievements, the example of their institutional (and personal) body language is also very powerful.[9] A lot of influence is exerted by these almost imperceptible means, some of it deliberate and socially desirable, and some not.

It is possible for institutions to organise ethos, just as they can consciously construct social capital, but it is difficult. It is like trying to make a team out of a set of self-regarding players. There has to be some sharing of identity if ethos is to be strong. In short, the institution has to become an identity-group for the majority of those associated with it. This works very like a family when it acts as a family-identity group, as discussed in Chapter 6. This institutional family will build and consolidate its identity through stereotypes, rules, rituals, joint reflections, symbols and narratives which the institution will have to promote and spread actively.[10]

In Figure 7.2 all the groups shown in the inner boxes will need to be members of the identity group, if the ethos is to be important

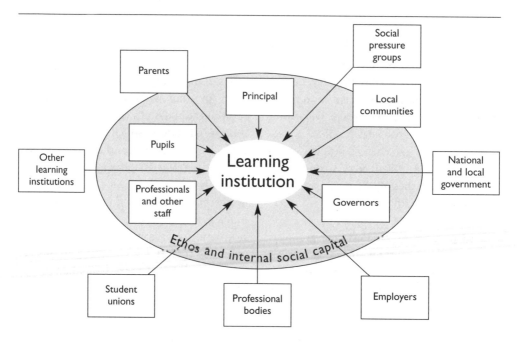

Figure 7.2 Institutional ethos and social capital

in the motivational story. Parents and local communities (shown on the edge) will need to recognise and support it, if not actually join.

If an institution is to have a distinctive ethos, it needs to consider very carefully what to create, and how to create and sustain it, and it cannot expect to do it out of a manual. If the group identity includes strong elements relevant to motivational development, it will strongly reinforce the effectiveness of the motivational influence which an institution can muster. All the large scale motivating forces of group-feeling will become available.

Whether the establishing of a motivational ethos would be a good thing or not depends on the nature of the relevant skills, and the favoured strategies and actions which the influence seeks to support. Well-supported motivation is not inherently right, of course. Independent schools based on ancient foundations tend to have a strong ethos, for

example, and much of it affects the motivation of their students profoundly. But whether the motivation always attaches to things that are appropriate to the UK in the 21st century is vigorously contested.

Identity group or coalition
As in the case of the family, the identity group contrasts with a view of the organisation as a loose, possibly uneasy, coalition of the people and groups who make it up, combined in negotiation, professional activity and all kinds of power play. As an identity group, the institution is a corporate entity. It has corporate efficacy and corporate assessments of value, as if the institution in all its parts has a jointly-held motivation. In contrast, a loose coalition has no corporate features – just individual motivations, reflecting all the different interests bound up in the organisation.[11]

The tendency of identity group members to converge on the group stereotype means that the motivations of individual members converge onto a group-motivation.[12] This, in a general sense, is the institution's own motivational narrative. It is a corporate view. Formalized constitutional devices within the group – such as voting and discussion – help to crystallize the group view out of convergent, individual motivations, and to legitimize the outcome.

Individual members will support the corporate view, and act upon it publicly, even though, if pressed, they are able to see a distinction between their personal view and the group-ordained view. Politicians are often seen to be wrestling with just this sort of ambivalence when talking about collective responsibility. Even in the closest entity group, individuals can drop out of the corporate view back into their individual group member's view (their we-motivation) – or, going further, into their lone individual's viewpoint (I-motivation). From one moment to another, as saliency switches, outside influencers may find themselves talking to a principal who is taking the official line as representative of the institution's corporate self – the body with the ethos; or to someone who is clearly thinking as an individual, but one who is personally committed to the organisation; or to a disgruntled head, thinking of retirement.

Outside influences

Figure 7.2 shows an institution which has organised its internal motivational arrangements, and developed its social capital and its ethos. But there are still outside influences to consider, beyond the institutional boundaries. There are four main factors, all acting within the wider cat's cradle of motivational forces: peer institutions; employers and the labour market; various social pressure groups; professional bodies and unions; and national and local government. Parents and local communities, if not bound into the institution itself, may also be regarded as outside influencers. All these can condition what the institution might achieve in motivational matters, in much the same way as commercial forces, jobs and income impinge on the motivational activities of the family. Some outsiders may wish to gain influence by joining the identity group, so that they can influence the corporate motivation from the inside – parents and representatives from local communities, for example. Others – including government, social pressure groups or employers – will normally try to influence from the back seat without joining.

The external context really does matter. As an institution's principal and governors try to establish their ethos, and to galvanise the internal motivational chain to the students, through all categories of the staff, they find that their hands are tied and their actions conditioned by wider accountabilities and constraints in the cat's cradle. Sometimes these can help, but they may also hinder.

Little is known about some of these outside forces. What leverage do professional bodies and unions exert on institutions' motivational activities? What arrangements are there for institutions to help each other in motivational matters? How big an impact do social interest groups – like Amnesty International or Greenpeace – or political parties, or even religious groups, really have? Ignorance about the size and nature of such outside forces is deep-seated.

National government is a key outsider, particularly in the state-funded sector of education. It applies funds, regulates quality, prescribes curricular content, directs educational methods, maintains qualification structures, sets targets, controls pay and conditions for teachers, regulates aspects of professional conduct, and controls the competition and co-operation between institutions, among other things. Its policies and regulations also influence other important players affecting learning institutions, such as local government, religious bodies and – increasingly – commercial organisations. Its influence reaches deep into learning institutions, right down to the motivation and motivational development of individual learners. Beyond the motivational influence of the family, these interventions are the most profound within the institutional environment. They have the most direct effect on an institution's scope to shape individuals' motivation for learning.

Much of this intervention is in the name of democratic accountability for money spent, and, in some cases, of giving something in return for the removal of freedom which compulsory education implies. But the curious thing about it is that government, for all its schemes and tools, does not spell out clearly what its motivational policies are in terms of content, or systems and procedures, or even statistical monitoring. There are no surveys of motivation, and therefore no targets or aims relating directly to measures of motivation.

This is strange because successive governments have presided over arrangements for initial education which have a very clear, well documented and fundamental motivational effect. These arrangements deliberately separate and sift the population using academic criteria to sort them into successful and not-successful.[13] By doing so government divides the learning motivation of the population into three more or less equal groups creating: a selected learning élite which tends to perpetuate itself over generations; a rump of demotivated learners, who are almost permanently switched off from formal learning; and a semi-motivated middle portion.[14] Recent attempts to address this motivational problem, through the reorganization of national administration and some increased funding for adult learning, will have benefited some individuals; but it will have done nothing to counter the underlying cause.

There is no way for the electorate to know whether governmental silence on motivational matters means that the government (of whatever colour) approves of this state of affairs but does not wish to own up to it; or that it is hiding behind output targets and other paraphernalia, because it does not know how to improve the motivational result; or that it thinks that clear motivational policies are actually impossible, and that the educational arrangements must be designed and run rather like the American constitution – to prevent any one particular interest having too strong a grip on the steering wheel.

These are matters of national policy. Closer to home are many issues of inconsistent and ineffective direction, within the measures which government does promote. In schools, for example, the establishment of a national curriculum as a principle gives some basic assurance that young people will not be denied a basic education. That is presumably meant to be motivating. But it also has huge implications for institutions' and professionals' ability to galvanize children to lifelong learning strategies. What is more, the detailed specification of a National Curriculum is immensely damaging in its motivational effects. It eats into institutional time and professional flexibility, demoralizes staff and hamstrings their motivational influence.

State schools are already full of motivational inconsistencies of this kind. Some may reflect the dual role of schools as places to promote learning and as places charged with the job of schooling young people into socially acceptable behaviour. Over-emphasis on the latter favours an authoritarian atmosphere, encouraging normative – institutionalized – behaviour. It is a fine line between learning to toe the line in the interests of social harmony, and docile acceptance of organisational intent. The latter is increasingly evident among UK students rounding off their initial education in colleges and universities. None of this promotes the creativity and innovation that gives people hope, and that will enable the UK to hold its own in the world economy.

A clear national policy framework for learning motivation is needed, dealing with the spin-off difficulties and motivational inconsistencies associated with government interventions in learning institutions.

Communities

The second motivational environment to be examined here is community. In this discussion it is defined as the set of social environments outside the family, education and the work place. This is where the person, whose motivation is the centre of attention, meets people as more or less free-standing individuals, and as members of groups.

Groups include identity groups and interest groups (coalitions of interest), which reflect people's subjective categorisation of them-

selves and their interests. Other groupings, which we are hardly concerned with here, are based on objective statistics, such as people who own computers or overweight six-year-olds. An individual will typically belong to a number of these groups at the same time, some temporarily and some permanently. Certain groups, particularly identity groups, will tend to be at odds with each other and seek to favour their own members against out-groups. Some others may have a co-operative or benign relationship with other groups.

Free-standing individuals are likely to be group members too, but are defined here as people in the social environment who exert a motivational influence in their personal capacity, and not as members of any group(s). Such people include friends and acquaintances, mentors, media-promoted role models, and chance encounters. They can offer support with their motivational skills, as well as influence others towards particular acts and behaviours. When they do so one-to-one they construct a special group of two, the influenced and the influencer – and vice versa, if the relationship is mutual. Such identity pairing can have a powerful impact on an individuals' motivation – sometimes for good, and sometimes not.

David Mulcahy was bullied at school because he was small for his age. John Duffy was bullied at school because he had bright red hair. They formed a mutually supportive group of two, developing a shared fascination with violence. Over a period of years they plotted and carried out a series of attacks on women, starting with rape and escalating to murder on several occasions. John Duffy was jailed in 1988. Years later he gave evidence against David Mulcahy, who was jailed in 2001. [15]

Social influence of individuals
Community has a particularly important motivational role to play in the lives of individuals whose families or other social groups do not provide the support they need. The more articulated a social network is, and the more weak links it has, the easier it will be for such individuals to find others who can fulfil a motivational role.[16] A weak link is established where individuals are merely distantly acquainted, but nevertheless are able to use the contact as a route to other people who may help with a problem. This may happen more or less informally, as in the case of the village postmaster who helps illiterate pensioners by reading their post to them; or it may be formalised through organisations such as the Samaritans, or Amnesty International, which exist to organise weak links supporting the motivation of individuals.

In the learning domain the question is whether there is room for similar networking arrangements based on altruism and mutual benefit between individuals and between groups?[17] Such possibilities immediately take the argument back to schools and the family, where most of the job of building a sense of social responsibility has to be accomplished. Yet only lately has a very small element of citizenship education entered the national curriculum, which might begin to address this need.[18]

Influence of groups
Lone individuals apart, Figure 7.3 shows the wider groups, and their motivational influence. The statistical groups are of little interest here, and so drop out.

The question is how this complex environment of groups influences individual members' motivation to learn. The influence is felt both at project level and in learning strategy, and makes its mark both in the development of the person's motivational knowledge, processes and skills, and in the creation of motivation for particular activities. The overall effect is substantial, and in

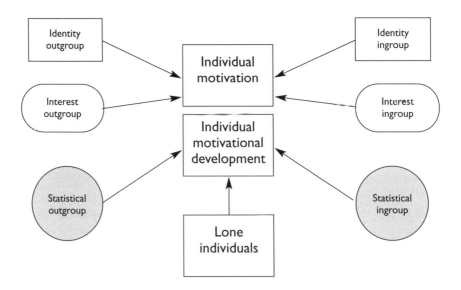

Figure 7.3 Influence of wider groups

particular cases may be greater than that of family and other influencing environments.

Figure 7.4 sets out the questions to be addressed. They are broadly similar to those already considered in relation to the family and the learning institution and we will see similar ones also in the workplace environment.

First there are questions about how a particular group influences individual member's specific motivation or motivational development. Next come questions about the group itself: how it marshals its own motivation, and how it develops its own motivational skills to have an impact on individual members. Then there are the true outsiders, who apply leverage on the group in order to influence individual members at one remove. At that level there are issues about how the leverage is applied and what generates the will to apply it.

Group influences on members – The how questions can be answered in terms of the same list of factors as those described in the family environment. On the developmental front are efforts to influence personality, motivational meta-knowledge and assessment skills, and learning skills themselves. On the specific motivation front are role-models, packaged attitudes, encouragement, criticism, etc. (see Figure 6.1, page 66, for both categories). All leave a large mark, and their effect depends on how far each member's motivational assessments are pieced together from gobbets of conventional wisdom, or are thought through carefully from scratch.

These interventions are normally and mainly undertaken by established group members, in the name of the group. This is analogous to the peer pressure inside education, or sibling help in the family. But there may be an important role for specialist group members

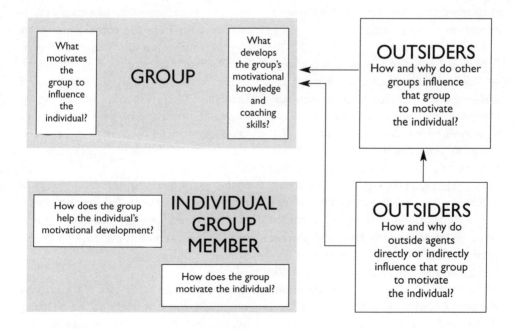

Figure 7.4 Questions about group influence

or leaders, analogous to parents or teachers – different groups organise things differently.[19] There will also be an important role for social capital as a general back-up for the motivational influencing.[20] This too can be organised, fostered and exploited.

Organisation of groups – It is on this point of organisation that the distinction between identity groups and interest groups becomes very important.[21]

Suppose officials at a religious centre (which we shall call a church for convenience, but it could be a chapel, synagogue or mosque) want to build the sense of an identity group among those who use it regularly. Beyond inspiring members to learn specific matters of doctrine, they may also decide to help them to increase their individual learning motivation more generally by helping them to improve their motivational meta-knowledge and assessment skills. Where will the motivation to carry this mission forward come from, in such a case?

Following the earlier argument, the church will have the job of somehow bringing together the we-motivations of its individual members into a corporate view, and it will have more or less developed processes for doing this. The fruits of the process will then become the official view, backed by the official motivation. The church community, as a corporate body, has certain knowledge and skills at its disposal. By an extended sense, it has its own motivational process at project and strategy level delivering corporate energy to build and harness the resources needed, and then to undertake the instructional task. If corporate efficacy is low, and if the corporate view of net value is low, the church's performance will

be lacklustre.[22] If the opposite is true, the group will be keen as mustard.

Members will be expected to apply the official motivation, and – by the usual dynamics of converging on the stereotype – members will progressively fall in behind it. The answer to the question of where the church's motivation comes from, and how it raises its performance in reaching corporate motivational positions, will therefore lie in the formal and informal processes of democracy and leadership in the body of the church. The more the group consolidates the corporate view in its narratives and rituals, the more strongly will the current of corporate motivational energy flow.

The individual members, on the other hand, will still have – somewhere on the backburner – an individual we-motivation about their church getting involved in promoting learning among its members (including themselves), and they will fall back on this if saliency shifts from the corporate view to their personal group view. They may fall back even further, if saliency shifts to the I-motivation associated with a different self altogether. Their responses will be largely shaped by the altruism they have for net value experienced by other members, and the costs which fall on them personally.

In the entity group, therefore, the ways in which the members fashion corporate motivation will strongly condition how it sets about organising its influencing activities in support of learning.

What is more, as in the case of the learning institution, there is likely to be a strong ethos within the group which saturates the activities of its members, with common

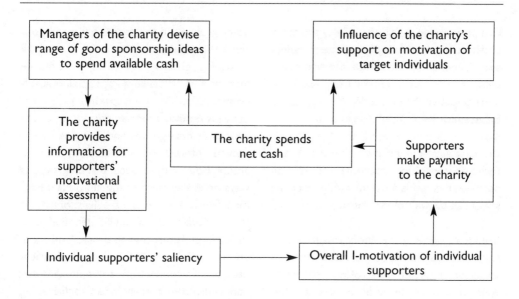

Figure 7.5 Motivation in a charity-based interest group

assumptions and values about how the corporate view is put into effect. Separate, but closely involved in ethos, will be social capital between the members.[23] This will also be a strong support for motivational influence. Whether these organisational consequences of group-motivation are a good thing or not depends on the basic aims of the group. Extremist groups, such as Scientologists, practise very tight and unquestioning forms of 'group think', which can seriously entrap group members.

An interest group will go about organising its group motivating activities quite differently.[24] Figure 7.5 takes the example of a charity group, which has supporters – perhaps even members – but which does not draw them into an identity relationship. The supporters simply use the charity as a convenience, jointly sharing the costs of a secretariat which will propose action options which they are likely to support. The charity is, therefore, like a bank for its members' individual altruism. The members never get

into a we-motivational mind-set at all, let alone a corporate view. In our example, the charity is interested in actively promoting schemes to motivate the public towards learning about race relations in a locality. For the charity's individual supporters, working through the organisation reduces the costs of finding options to address their altruistic interest in local social harmony. The lower costs increase their individual motivation to act, when their social conscience self is salient. But that is as far as it goes. They feel no significant loyalty for the charity. It is not part of their self-definition.

This is an example where co-operation enhances individual motivation of influencers, and the significance for learning motivation is clear: groups of this kind may support individual learning motivation for all sorts of purposes. They are devices to prompt and gather small amounts of altruism, scattered across a population, into a force which can make a difference through motivational influence.

Groups working in this sort of way are often charities, but increasingly they are partnerships between groups from the voluntary, public and private sectors of the economy. Their potential for supporting learning, either for itself, or as a means to other purposes, has hardly begun to be tapped. Even if individuals are making no current use of them, their existence for potential use has an option-value, and is an important part of the social capital available to those people.

Outsiders – We come finally to those outside interests, which prompt social groups to undertake motivating roles in particular ways or contexts. Figure 7.4 shows other groups, and other agents. All these are part of the wider cat's cradle of Figure 6.1.

The example of the church can illustrate this area as well. The church benefits from direct and specific relationships with other groups, and from external social capital relationships as well. For example, church officials might seek the co-operation of an environmental group, to inform and help a local residents' group in improving their environment. In this case the relationship is based on a negotiation of interest for each party, rather than from some assimilation of two groups into a new superordinate identity-group.[25] Skilled social entrepreneurs – a relatively rare commodity in the UK – are usually needed to stitch these sorts of relationships together for mutual benefit, and religious centres are well placed to provide the base for such entrepreneurship.[26]

In terms of social capital, the degree of background motivational stimulus which a group can get from other groups outside depends on whether the social capital is a positive rather than negative asset, and on the proximity of

other groups and the degree and conditionality of their support. Networks of mutually sustaining groups can strongly reinforce motivational influence among their individual members. The extent to which this works depends on the corporate motivation of the various identity groups, and/or the common pooled interest of members of interest groups. Both of these depend in their various ways on the altruism of the individual members. This is the crucial ingredient, which it is the particular role of families, learning institutions, political organisations, and faith groups to fashion. On this depends the richness of interconnectivity and mutuality that community development aims to achieve.

Employers and government are other important outsiders. Employers can become heavily involved in groups through sponsorship or targeted advertising.[27] A brewing firm, may sponsor a football team in order to appeal to an informal group of football enthusiasts. Introducing their brand of beer into the rituals of the identity group is meant to motivate the members towards that particular brand and associated lifestyle. Such devices can have important motivational consequences for learning. They help to fuel a culture of antisocial laddishness, which is deeply hostile to the cause of learning motivation. There is, of course, the possibility that the influence can cut the other way: commercial interests can gain by creating an image of themselves as socially responsible; and sometimes it may literally be in their interest to stimulate particular bits of learning or learning strategy. The cumulative effect of commercial pressures of this kind working through community groups is substantial.[28]

Government can do much to stimulate groups to foster learning motivation. A certain hesitancy in doing so derives from the general obscurity of governmental purposes regarding motivation, and from the fear that groups will run out of control and put public money at risk. Successive governments have invested heavily in the bid-culture, where groups and organisations have to compete to bid for short term, often small, packets of public money in order to run experimental community projects, in learning or in other fields of social policy. This has very serious drawbacks, not least in producing severe demotivation on the part of hardworking community development workers who find themselves trapped in such a system.[29]

At the same time, governments have not been very active in promoting social entrepreneurship; or in promoting new ways of fostering altruism relating to community through schools or other means;[30] or in finding new ways to pool altruism in the community to support learning and other public objectives. On the contrary, successive governments have fostered strong individualistic policies in many fields, and have withdrawn many long established local delegations and local responsibilities, which served as a matrix for developing community mutuality. All these have meant that the combined thrust of social groupings and organisations in support of learning motivation has fallen far short of what is both possible and needed.

Employers

The world of work is the last environment to be examined in this chapter. Its influence is central in the story of learning motivation. We need to look at how employers create motivation to learn for the skills they require to compete in global product markets. But

we also need to see how their activities influence learning motivation in their roles as sellers of goods and services, many of which are rivals of learning.

Learning for skills
Figure 7.6 shows the dynamics of motivation for skills learning in the workplace environment. Figure 7.7 shows the labour market for economically active people, whether they are employed or unemployed; and the learning market for skills, which abuts onto the labour market. All these have an impact on motivation for learning skills in the world of work.

Workplace: Figure 7.6 compares with the similar diagram for learning institutions, Figure 7.1. It shows a chain of influence through specific acts intended to motivate:

• Managers can play a role akin to teachers in learning institutions – seeking to motivate specific learning at lower staff levels, spreading general motivational knowledge, and coaching for improvements in motivational assessment skills.

• Fellow workers can play a very important part in motivating individual workers, just as peer groups influence students in the world of education, and members do in groups. Employers can support this role by positive measures. Fellow workers can also exert an oppositional influence, particularly if the employer is viewed with suspicion. Fellow workers may organise in unions and staff associations for this and other purposes.

• At higher level, the employer can ensure that managers are motivated to undertake this role, and have the meta-knowledge

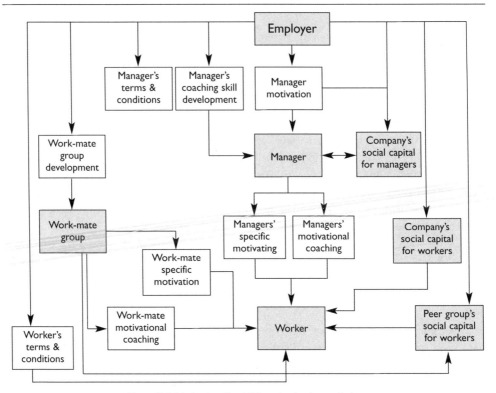

Figure 7.6 Motivation for skill learning in the workplace

about motivation and good motivational coaching skills, to pass on to workers. Managers' motivation, like that of parents and teachers, is very important. It draws on assessments of net value and probability, and is subject to helplessness and other coping responses in the event of difficulty.

These specific acts can be supported by building and maintaining general social capital inside the workplace, and by specialised forms of social capital, appropriate to particular categories of recipient. In effect, colleagues can provide a motivational reserve army to support employees at all levels informally, as need arises.[31] Social capital for employers themselves lies largely outside, in their contacts with other employers in the same locality and similar lines of work, and in trade associations and industrial bodies.

Figure 7.6 underlines one particular feature which has not been emphasised in the other environments: the use of terms and conditions of employment as a motivator, both for managers and for workers. This centres on the use of pay and monetary inducements to secure motivation for particular actions.[32] Properly applied, it can be very flexible, including: time off; choice of learning mode; enhancements for job satisfaction; promotional prospects; recognition of status, and much else. These can give the employer considerable leverage on all aspects of motivation. Alongside these, and contrasting strongly, are motivational influences by fiat and order, under pain of various sanctions. These can work to a degree in the short term, but have a long-term drawback in the form of loss of self-esteem for the recipient.

The employer presides over this hierarchical system of motivational influence, although not necessarily controlling every part. A few employers will have a fully articulate and monitored motivational policy, involving learning or other aspects of workforce behaviour. But many will not. In the UK there is a tendency for employers to view the workplace as a collaborative – but essentially contractual – environment, where individuals are induced to put their energies into production in exchange for remuneration, job satisfaction, status, and (increasingly) personal development. This sort of workplace is equivalent to an interest group, as defined earlier. Such arrangements are a delicate balance of advantage or disadvantage between worker and employer, and have the capacity to turn sour if the balance shifts.

Some employers, inclining towards the Japanese collectivist model, will try to move the psychological contract between employer and worker onto an identity group footing.[33] Here the workplace functions more like a family or identity-group in the community, with loyalties which supersede personal interest. As in other contexts, this means that the motivations of individual workers, as expressed in their salient self as 'worker' or 'trade unionist', will switch over to we-motivation centred on the enterprise. These are still individual motivations, but may converge on stereotypical norms, and may eventually be assimilated into a corporate view.

Given skilled management and good will, this psychological shift can produce a learning organisation, where the workplace will buzz with motivation to learn and to develop motivational skills. This is where the employee development scheme, on the Ford (EDAP) model fits in so well.[34] The energies released by this can be a winning recipe in the product markets. The conditions for the switch-over are not cheap, however: a higher commitment to workers' interests than to shareholders' short-term profits, akin to what is normal in families; the removal of threats and inessential power play; consultation; abolition of excessive competition and status distinctions inside the organisation; egalitarian norms; altruistic and empathetic behaviour by managers; and new rituals, norms and narratives applied by all, to all.

Labour market and outside factors: In the cases of the family, learning institutions and the community we have seen how external factors play a role in spurring on the motivational activities which these bodies apply to their individual members. The same is true for employers.

Apart from government, the main links are with the product markets, in the UK and overseas. Figure 7.7 shows how the employer links to the outside world. In this case, the employing organisation is taken to be in the private sector and commercial in its aims.

The figure shows the employer assessing the product market environment and shaping its business plan accordingly. The plan requires a flow of skilled labour services, of given mix and quantity. The question is where the skills needed can be obtained. There are two routes: the inside track, where an employer can train up existing staff and redeploy

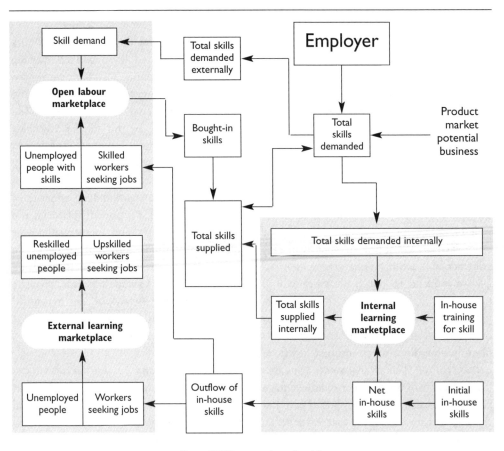

Figure 7.7 Three markets for skills

workers to meet the mix of skills needed, removing workers whose skills or potential no longer fit the plan; and the outside track, where new workers with the necessary skills or potential are recruited and inducted for a price. The balance between these tracks is a key part of the employer's human resources plan, which is itself a key part of the business plan.

• On the inside track, in-house training and redeployment costs have to be set against substantial recruitment costs and induction training for new recruits, and the risks involved in hiring new workers whose performance is a little-known quantity. But the balance can greatly affect the chances of an

employer maintaining the workforce as an identity group. Japanese firms have shown that an in-house bias is more likely to promote the identity milieu (in the UK, as well as in Japan). The terms and conditions offered to internal trainees will be a major extrinsic motivator for the learning of in-house staff.

• On the outside track, the employer will have to pay wages and offer conditions according to the rates set in the labour market, with the likelihood that any bidding up of wage costs, etc. will have to be paid out to existing staff as well. Part of the staff recruited in this way will come from other firms, causing attrition of existing labour stocks in those firms; and vice versa. The rest will come from unemployed people of appropriate experience, or from unemployed people or staff in employment somewhere, who have used the learning market to change their skills to suit the market need.

The potential flow of new staff out of the labour market and into jobs provides, at one remove, a stimulus to the learning market to reskill or upskill people to meet demand. Job offers on the open labour market are crucial to the extrinsic motivation which people who are looking for work have for learning relevant skills.

It can, of course, be risky for learners to participate in speculative learning for hire in the open labour market as inexperienced first timers. Careers guidance services exist to help individuals respond to the signals given off by employers, both those in employment and also those flagged in the open market. The existence of good business planning on the one hand and good careers guidance on the other strengthens motivation to learn on the speculative route, because both reduce uncertainty for the learner.[35]

We now come to the critical issue. If the employer does not take a vigorous approach to opportunities in the product markets, the internal system for learning motivation is likely to sag disastrously, and the chances of reaching an identity-group approach to the psychological contract will be blown. Moreover, the external market signals given to the labour market, and at one remove to the learning market, will be weak and indistinct, and the effectiveness of the labour market in redeploying the national labour force will be greatly diminished.

In short, there has to be a firm grip on the external markets if the distribution of the economic incentives to learn productive skills is to work well. This is where the employer's strategy is important. The employer may assume that skill shortages and labour problems are endemic, so that it is a waste of time trying to trade at the leading edge in high skill product markets. In this case the business will gradually drift downhill, sticking to standard product lines or services run on obsolete technology, while international competitors chase the new opportunities. This is the classic scenario of the 'low skill equilibrium', and is the employers' version of the individual's 'going through the motions' response to coping difficulties. It has been the besetting problem in much of British manufacturing.[36]

Wrapped up in this failure of will is another important difficulty. This arises where an employer approaches the job of working out a rational plan for his or her skills with preconceived rules of thumb which are inadequate to finding the best course of action.[37] Two basic corporate attitudes continue to trap the unwary:
• a traditional unwillingness among employers to pay for training of their own staff, because they see training costs as a saveable current cost on the profit and loss account, and also because they make the unrealistic assumption that trained workers do not have to be paid more money as their productivity grows. If the share price has to be sustained in the short term by profit results which impress the stock market, training – for them – is the place to look for cuts;
• a similar traditional unwillingness to invest in training in-house because employers think that trained workers will leave for higher wages elsewhere. Studies show that

this fear of poaching is commonly exaggerated, and fails to see the link between good training activities inside the organisation and recruiting good staff in the first place.[38] If employers collectively are looking more towards the open labour market for the skills they need than to their own provision they are likely to be disappointed, unless the government steps in to pay for speculative training.

These difficulties mean that employing organisations can and do suffer from key motivational hang-ups in the heart of their high level business planning. Short sightedness, heavy risk discounting, and low corporate efficacy assumptions all weaken the motivation the organisation needs to press its case with vigour in product markets and in the markets for skills. If there is this rot at the centre, the arrangements the organisation makes for feeding motivational influence through management to the workforce – however constituted – will have no lifeblood in them. This is directly analogous to the school which has no ethos; or the community which has no collective identity; or the family which has given way to chaos on motivational matters.

What lies behind many of the difficulties over learning in the workplace are the so-called 'rules of the game' regarding who pays for learning.[39] For example, it is generally expected that employers will pay for new skills if employees will not be able to transfer them easily to other employers (such as using highly specified software). At the same time, many employers, fearful of poaching, are unwilling to pay for skills which have a degree of transferability and prefer to buy in the skills on the open labour market. What is more, employers are often unwilling to pay for basic literacy and numeracy, arguing that it is the state's job to pay for those skills. In many cases they would also be unwilling to pay for general education.

Workers also have rules of thumb. For example, they often expect the state to supply, free of charge, any learning which is needed in the workplace which their employer is unwilling or unable to pay for. They have been used to free education when young, and extrapolate that into adulthood. They also expect the employer to pay in full for any learning which the organisation requires or compels.

The extrinsic element of motivation to learn work-related skills depends not only on how employers distribute their skill needs between internal and external markets, but also on who picks up the bill for the costs. The 'rules of the game' conventions influence this in significant ways. But they tend to be rather loose presumptions or cultural norms, used by employers' and workers' representatives to by-pass negotiation on learning matters. Rarely are they clearly stated or firmly agreed between employer and worker representatives, or between both of these parties and the government.

This brings out an important point about government, as another external source of leverage on the employer. Governments have not helped to clarify the rules of the game. In many instances they have put the cost of skills onto employers; but in other cases they have paid the full cost through state budgets. There is little rhyme or reason about this. What is more, while the state has sponsored the Investors in People standard in an attempt to strengthen the ways in which firms establish extrinsic motivation to learn inside and outside employment, it has not ensured that this scheme has wide coverage.[40] It has also failed to tackle the accounting problems and fears of poaching which lie at the heart of so much employer reluctance to invest in skills. This lack of cogency in public policy in motivating people towards skills learning for the world of work is very reminiscent of the situation in education and in community development.

Employers as purveyors of consumption and lifestyle

Employers who operate in consumer markets also have a very important effect on learning through the goods and services they sell and, in particular, through the lifestyle advertising and promotion they undertake. Figure 7.8 indicates the wide reach of this influence, propagated in consumer markets through the cat's cradle.

An employing organisation gives out various messages, either directly to individuals; or via intermediaries who may add spin of their own – amplifying, stifling, or otherwise playing Chinese Whispers by a variety of means:

• If the employer is in the learning business then the messages will directly address recipients' learning motivation.

• If the employer is in a business competitive with learning – spending money on changing your car just for the sake of fashion, for example – the intended effect will be to influence recipients' motivation towards

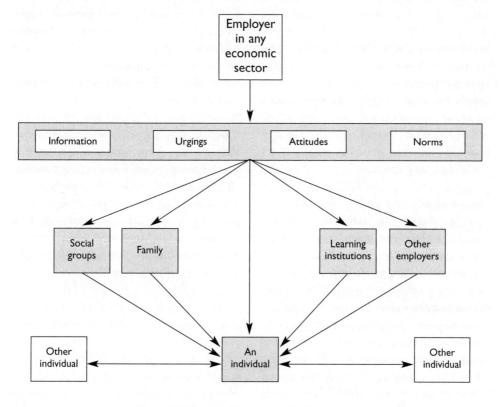

Figure 7.8 The potential reach of effective marketing

the alternatives, and therefore away from learning options.

- If the employer is in a business complementary to learning, the effect will be to stimulate learning motivation indirectly, via other goods or services – the effect of foreign holidays on eating habits and foreign language learning, for example.

Research has been done into how such messages can be made to attract recipients' attention and mental processing.[41] Subliminal emotional cueing, for example, is important – associating the feel-good factor with a product or service. So also is the in-group/ out-group origin of the message. If the message comes from the salient in-group, but is the expected party line, it may be routinely approved, but not be focused on particularly.

In matters like this, learning providers – who are also employers selling their wares in an increasingly competitive market – are well behind the sophisticated influencing widely deployed by organisations which are primarily commercial. Studies are needed into how appropriate improvements can be made. Learning providers and community groups need to be very clear what they are doing if they accept sponsorship from commercial undertakings. The force of the promotion may cut directly against their wider aims, or ethos, or their own motivational activities among their members.

More generally, promoting consumption to individuals, directly or indirectly, is very significant for motivation to learn, in respect of both projects and strategies. It makes its impact on identity groupings and lifestyle choices, as well as on particular goods and services. Commercial impact may sometimes enhance learning motivation. But it is more likely to be detrimental, both in the way that it diminishes the net value of learning projects and strategies, and in the way that it tightens budgets for time and money, at the expense of learning.

The invasion of minds can produce a situation where large employers who win recognition for their fine training records and their enlightened learning policies actually undermine learning motivation in the wider population, through excessive stimulation of anti-learning lifestyles and spending behaviour – all in the pursuit of short-term profits for shareholders.[42] In the longer run this is unlikely to be in the interests of commercial survival.

There is little sign that government is yet able or willing to control forces such as these through more extensive regulation, or to provide some countervailing pressure – perhaps through advertising of its own to put the record straight on behalf of learning, or through the content of the National Curriculum – which will help rising generations to be more critical.

Notes and references (Numbers refer to publications listed in the Reference section)

[1] See 4, compared to 28; also 192.

[2] See Freire 90 for warning about teachers assuming oppressive power roles

[3] See Freire 90.

[4] See 83 for a useful way of measuring school/teacher/parent interactions.

[5] See Moll et al 175.

[6] See 150.

[7] See Slavin 218, and Johnston & Johnston 147; also Clark 41 and Hertz-Lazarowitz.

[8] See 193.

[9] See Bandura 9.

[10] See 148.

[11] The literature of social movements is suggestive here. See the analysis of feminism and trade union activism in 154.

[12] See Brown 31, and Hogg & Abrams 141.

[13] See Smith & Spurling 220. Also the authoritative study by Sargant 207.

[14] See 21 for an official survey.

[15] This is a real case.

[16] See 63.

[17] See 76 and 82.

[18] See Crick 49.

[19] See Kelly and Breinlinger 154.

[20] See Schuller & Burns 208.

[21] See 34 for an authoritative survey; also 148.

[22] Bandura has begun the task of refining this concept of group efficacy: see 10.

[23] See Coleman in 120 for the case of organization of traders in a bazaar.

[24] See 181, and discussion in 154.

[25] A superordinate group is a large group subsuming smaller groups. See Brown 31.

[26] Social entrepreneurs have been studied by Demos.

[27] See Smith & Spurling 222 for analysis of a company's motivation.

[28] See 37.

[29] See Williamson 246 for a devastating brief analysis of the bid culture.

[30] See Clark 41 and 73.

[31] See Digenti 66.

[32] See review by Deci et al 62.

[33] For ground-breaking studies of the psychological contract see Guest & Conway 115 and 116; also 95. See Park 184 for analysis of compulsion in training activity. See Ashton & Green 8 for useful descriptions of different motivational business cultures; also Hoffstede 139.

[34] See 17 and 186; also important is Eraut et al 80.

[35] See 48.

[36] See Booth and Snower 29 for a comprehensive survey; also Oulton 183 for an example and 58.

[37] The Investors in People standard provides the outline model for this. See 227.

[38] Green 109 gives an authoritative review. See also 228.

[39] See 145 for the general climate of organizational change in these matters.

[40] See 227.

[41] See 157, 189 & 231.

[42] See 7.

Chapter 8:
Policy implications

Introduction

This final chapter reviews the policy implications of this journey through the motivation landscape. That journey began by exploring how motivation works in humans, and how individuals manage it through projects expressing a hierarchy of long-term and short-term goals. The argument then shifted to the environments which nurture this individual motivation, where a range of stakeholders sustain and bend it this way and that. We saw how these influencers can manipulate individual motivation to learn, but also how they can influence each others' efforts, sometimes supporting and sometimes interfering. These efforts form a cat's cradle of interactive forces, all pushing and pulling with incentives, disincentives and compulsions, to affect individual motivation.

Figure 8.1 summarizes the complex cross-linkage in a way which highlights three important aspects.

• The first point is the pervasive influence of globalization in society and the economy, shown in the background to Figure 8.1.[1] Much of this influence is exerted through the role of commercial employers as sellers of goods and services, many of which are competitors to learning. But its influence also bears importantly on learning institutions, communities, families, and government.

• The second point is the role of government, whose influence extends within and around the cat's cradle. It has the job of trying to produce a sensible, if not optimal, balance of influence overall, while itself having its arm twisted by the other parties, and itself wanting to influence individual motivation in particular ways.

• The third crucial aspect is the overall balance of influence which, combined with the motivational inputs of individuals themselves, produces results in terms of the volume and mix of learning. This is shown in the centre of the figure, relating to the needs of individuals, families, employers and community.

The ultimate test of all the influencing and intervening which the stakeholders apply lies in the nature of this learning output: its size, content, relevance and moral value. This boils down in the end to the criterion of minimising regret over lifetimes of experience, taking a forward-looking, community perspective. Can people build and express the learning motivation in ways which make most sense of their potential for living good lives – as individuals and as members of communities, both for present and future generations? In these terms, have their lives been without regret? As far as the influencers are concerned, as they stretch and strain in their cat's cradle of influence, do

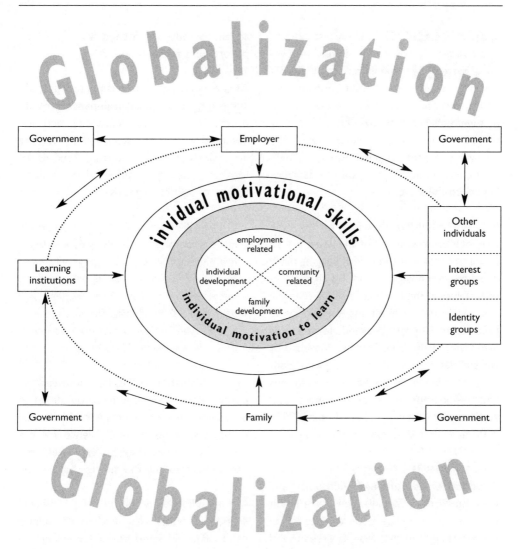

Figure 8.1 Cross-linkages affecting learning motivation

they realise the full effect of what they are doing in these terms? How far are their efforts mutually reinforcing, or do they cancel each other out? In particular, is government clear about its role, and does it have any particular rationale for its influence?

At this point we could all give up and go home to do more research. So little is known systematically about the cat's cradle and its effects, in terms of this fundamental test, that clear answers could be ruled out of the question. In truth, at the beginning of the 21st century, there is still virtually no motivational data, and only scant information on volumes of learning by type of purpose for anybody to use.[2]

Moreover, even if the data were there, a problem of interpretation would still remain. Would the data reflect a stable equilibrium of all the forces competing and co-operating in the cat's cradle? Or would it just indicate a temporary outcome of a national motivational system in permanent, unstable flux? If it were the latter, this would condemn the agents to ceaseless corrective action to protect and enhance their own interest and, by the same token, would render useless any overview of the results. Any overview attempted would be yet another destabilising jolt to the system.

It is very tempting therefore to take the road of more research. But the issues are so important that – at the risk of begging many questions and problems – in this chapter we offer a view in the context of global changes, and show the implications for policy in broad terms. A possible agenda for action is presented at the end. This overview is not yet sufficiently supported by empirical findings, but it has been tested in consultations and workshops with practitioners and academics in various fields during 1999–2000, and is available for further critique.

Global context

Powerful forces surround individuals and their motivation. Globalization – the result of a new world-wide economic order of free trade and capital flows – is a creature of liberal capitalist thinking, fed by massive changes in information flow, and by revolutions in communications media and technology.[3] The forces of globalization now threaten to run beyond the control of nation states and politicians. Its competitive structures and the unprecedented pace of change put jobs and workers at constant risk, setting them largely beyond the means of protection. It favours those who can master new information technologies, and who can think flexibly, outside the box, in diverse and innovative ways. Those who cannot do so are squeezed out, threatened by instability, poverty and social exclusion.[4]

As the world economy has opened up, consumption has seen rampant growth, promoted by lifestyle marketing and the commodification of society. Products are increasingly marketed through images of idealised lifestyles, rather than isolated images of particular goods.

Company A sells its clothing by filming it on a model who is wearing Company B's jewellery and loading Company C's luggage into the kind of car outside the kind of house in the sector of the market where Company A aspires to sell its clothing. The message is, "People who buy our clothes are successful enough to live like this".

The manipulation of fashion increases the effect, so that people want to be identified by fashionable logos (genuine or fake), even if they risk robbery and violence for the sake of the items they carry or wear, the cars they drive, and the houses they live in.

Commodification is the replacing of unpaid support services – a neighbour's helping hand, or family-based labour, for example – by goods or services bought in the market. Increasingly, individuals live independently, supported by technology and neglecting the needs and benefits of mutual community life. Seemingly, everything has to be bought and sold, and there is much less allocation of goods and services through traditional institutions, social channels and family structures. Social capital diminishes in parallel with this privatisation of living.

What is more, competition on a world scale, backed by the huge outreach of the media and marketing, is fuelling demand for customised products which are flexibly produced by just-in-time production methods.[5] The obverse of this production flexibility is the flexible labour market,[6] where the former dominance of men in employment has given way to a large increase in women's employment in the workplace – much of it reflecting improved educational opportunities for women.

But the dearth of genuinely family-friendly employment policies, combined with the effects of mobility expected of workers, is restructuring family life. It causes separations and loosens contact between generations, reducing time and opportunity for nurture and support. Using bought-in goods and services substitutes for mind-numbing chores, but it also reduces children's chances of learning domestic skills and crafts, and it feeds the commodification process. Capitalism now reaches right into the home, restructuring families just as it restructures businesses and jobs. It influences the different age groups with all-pervasive and increasingly sophisticated marketing, designed to maximise profits. Each group is segmented off, and assigned hyped-up and short-lived lifestyle identities – flagged up by the right logos and symbols – which then become the test of individuals' self-esteem.[7] Meanwhile, those without the wherewithal to buy the commodities are effectively marginalised.

Ulrich Beck has extended this picture.[8] He argues that a pall of apocalyptic thinking is now spreading over these workings of the globalised economy, that the limits of resources are in sight, and that the dangers of science-based pollution and environmental disaster on a planetary scale are now acknowledged by the very scientists who

expected populations to trust them. Mass protest rallies against corporate power, such as that at the Summit of World Leaders in Genoa in 2001, are a growing phenomenon. Belief in science is seen to be collapsing, and yet it is still needed to provide a critique of itself. The media's hunger for stories feeds a deep-seated, generalised anxiety which, in its turn, stokes the demand for constant news.

These changes are immense and apparently uncontrollable, yet the globalised system, and the risk society which attends it, accelerates ever faster, fuelled by relevant learning. The information, new technology, new production skills and marketing it depends on are all manifestations of work-related learning. The more such learning is fed in, the faster the carousel whirls, and the more learning individuals have to do to keep their balance. A sign of inflexibility at the wrong moment, and they will be spun out, irrespective of age or talent.

Those who protest that this is too bleak a picture cannot yet have had their means of livelihood whisked away to another part of the globe in the name of restructuring, by employers trying to maintain profit levels in ferocious world markets.[9] Plenty have. Effective response, at every level, depends on effective and lifelong motivation for learning.

Motivation at the start of the twenty-first century

This globalization is a predominant force on the whole structure of motivational influencing pressing in on the individual, and on individual learning in particular. Figure 8.2 summarizes some basic assessments of the damaging effects on the cat's cradle in its current form.

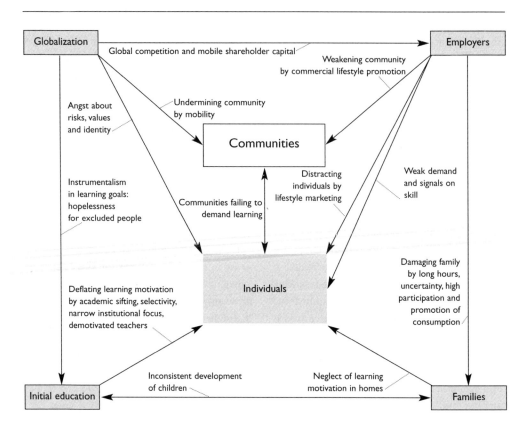

Figure 8.2 Damaging effects on learning motivation of the cat's cradle of influence

Employers

It is true that employers provide individuals and families with income, without which motivation to learn would be far weaker, and trade-offs between learning and necessary consumption would be biased towards the latter. But it comes with a major disadvantage: employers are under enormous pressures in rapidly globalizing product markets. Short-term shareholder value dominates corporate strategy, reclassifying any sentimental attachment to the specific labour force and local community as a luxury. Employers' demands for vastly increased flexibility in the labour market helps to destabilize families, by squeezing out time for non-work related learning, undermining

family group-identity, and turning households into highly contested arenas for negotiation. These developments are hostile to learning motivation among family members of any age, and are likely to be particularly felt in learning centred on personal, family and community development.

At the same time, employers are failing to articulate demands for skills to match the full extent of the opportunities inherent in a world market. If this were not so, individuals would have much stronger extrinsic motivation to learning for economically relevant skills. Moreover, the blitz of marketing and promotion, and the commodification of lifestyles launched by employers, weakens the possibility of individuals developing life-long learning strategies and identities to suit. So the world of work is cutting off its nose to spite its face. The labour force needs people who will build up and maintain high levels of flexible skills. If they are spending time and money doing that, can they also afford to develop lifestyles of high consumption, and have families, and invest time in developing learning in those families?

Family
Families have the prime responsibility for socialising young people towards learning. Families are very vulnerable to the risks and uncertainties of the job market, as indicated above. The increased mobility that responds to labour market demands reduces opportunities for building family social capital. Family identity is also under attack from the individualising effects of lifestyle marketing and commodification. A serious commitment of time and effort is needed just to pay for idealised homes/gardens/cars/holidays, or to keep fit in a stressful and polluted world. How much time is there left for family activities and learning?

This scenario encourages parents – however self sacrificial and well intentioned – to pass their motivational responsibilities on to crèches, child-minders and educational institutions. For families that either cannot afford or do not choose to do this, there is a strong temptation to get the children through school as quickly as possible, and into positions of (comparatively low level) earning power. In general, where parents' ambition for their children is not depressed by fatalism, learning tends to be defined according to the dominant goal of personal success through the formal educational route – that is, academic success. Children

are shepherded to and from school, and many are subsequently shepherded to and from organised after-school and weekend activities also. Much of their remaining time is catered for by technology, very often away from the rest of the family. More and more play involves choices offered by interactive technology, rather than the unlimited reach of the child's own imagination, inquisitiveness and experiment. On most days, family meals – which are important culturally as well as dietetically – have largely been replaced by individualised eating and grazing. Little family time remains for the role modelling of good relationships, nurturing, creativity, moral goodness, artistic understanding, altruism and social awareness, on which sound societies depend, and which schools have little time to touch.

These are strong currents in British society. Many parents strive for better than this against the odds, and good pilot schemes for family learning do exist. But they are shining lights in a sea of lost opportunity, threatened by the commodification of work and social life.

Educational institutions
Many parents see initial education as the chief socialising agent, and the main way that their children can, in due course, be launched into good jobs and self-sufficient consumption, on the back of good qualifications. This instrumentalist approach is reflected and amplified by government policy, and validated by global economic pressures. Given the choice, many families understandably try to allay the risks of global capitalism for their children by taking advantage of selective admission and narrowly focused routes through education. By definition, not all children can succeed in a selective system. So-called 'merit-based selection' –

based on technology or the arts or sport, for example – favours those children whose families are able to buy out-of-school coaching, just as academic selection does. The result is a weakening of the comprehensive principle on which educational effectiveness across the population depends. Whatever the basis, where there is selection there will be 'sink schools'.

The effect of this is to split the age cohort into three, near-enough equal, motivational segments: those at the top who have high motivation; those at the bottom who cannot compete educationally, and socially; and those in the middle, stranded between the two categories.[10]

Initial education is built round a specified National Curriculum, supported by a whole edifice of tests, targets and inspections. While structure and regulation are desirable, the strong instrumentalist bias of state education lays the foundation for learning which is predominantly focused on labour market needs.[11] Despite the rhetoric which surrounds UK schools, where every possibility is being pursued with some small pot of money or regulation, this instrumentalism actually does little or nothing of significance for the wider development of students, and their awareness of community and family interests and values. Above all it has very little effect in motivating students to adopt and pursue the wide, continuing and flexible learning strategies needed for effective social living and economic success in the longer term.

Many teachers still hold out for wider values such as these, against the forces of economic competitiveness which drive the schools. They feel threatened by policies which treat them primarily as administra-tors and technicians, and which undermine their motivation to teach well and to continue learning for themselves. Their social capital is seriously depleted, by personal stress and by competitive comparisons of professional performance. In many areas teachers would like to forge closer links with parents, but have scant resource and virtually no curriculum time or after-school hours opportunities to do so.[12] Inconsistencies abound between schools and parents, so that the developmental activities of each are undermined by the other.

Communities
Like families, communities are threatened by the capacity of globalization to undermine established values and structures through the constant flow of information – much of it via the unregulated internet. The labour market's demands for endless flexibility, which chops up and disposes of workers' time on a 24/7 basis, is aggressively anti-social. As long as there is little delegated authority, and a lack of social entrepreneurs to make essential links, it is no surprise that community potential remains so generally underdeveloped in the UK.

Influential identity-based organisations of the past – such as religions, trade unions or political parties – are increasingly squeezed out of people's lives by group activities based on consumption. Commercial investment advertises and maintains the various cultures, jargons, dress codes and rituals associated with a host of pastimes, such as clubbing, pubbing, off-roading and being a fan. These are important in the work hard, play hard culture of consumption. But the groups associated with them tend to be fragile, and vulnerable to the manipulation of fashion. They leave little room for non-commercial community interests, and ignore the more profound needs of the human mind and soul.

Currently too many individuals see little value in community, whether out of self-interest, or because community altruism and the sense of group identity is low; and many who do feel an underlying interest in community fail to combine effectively with others to undertake joint sponsorship of learning. They may believe that community arrangements are not effective, or distrust the political function, or shrink from the cost of finding useful coalitions in a chaotic situation.

The result is a failure to recognise the need for learning for community prosperity and security, or for other specific purposes.[13] Communities themselves are therefore handicapped in signalling learning needs to their individual members; they cannot easily engage people in community learning projects or strategies, using the strong motivations of salient group identity. There is a scattering of good community learning schemes, but the large potential is wasted on a substantial scale, with serious consequences for communities and individuals alike.

Motivation and the outputs of learning.

We now consider how these motivational dynamics affect the volume and mix of learning undertaken.

Mapping learning

Figure 8.3 shows how any learning can be classified in three broad ways, according to the kind of net value, expressed as expected

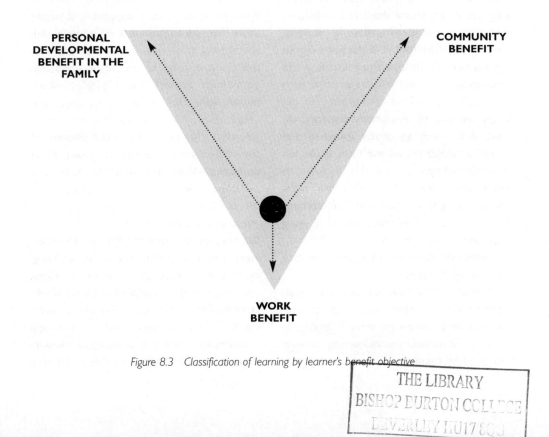

PERSONAL
DEVELOPMENTAL
BENEFIT IN THE
FAMILY

COMMUNITY
BENEFIT

WORK
BENEFIT

Figure 8.3   Classification of learning by learner's benefit objective

benefit for the learner:[14]
- in terms of labour market opportunities;
- through improved experience of community life, or as an expression of altruism;
- in the form of personal development – for the individual or for the family.

Learning may score under any of the three categories, and a learner can map any piece of learning – and indeed any learning strategy – subjectively somewhere in the triangle of benefits. The nearer a learning opportunity is mapped to any apex, the more important that goal is to the learner.

Unfortunately there is little or no evidence of a sufficiently wide definition to enable all the learning of the UK population to be classified in these terms. This is a fundamental deficiency in national statistics of learning. Although they have been much improved in recent years, there is still a long way to go before there is an adequate statistical basis for monitoring national learning achievement.[15] It is the net value to the learner that links lifelong learning and motivation.

In the absence of satisfactory statistics, we must work with anecdotal evidence and deduction. At this level the picture we see is dominated by:
- economic aspirations, which are highlighted in people's accounts of learning, and in official interpretations of lifelong learning;
- a utilitarian approach to learning among university students;
- a decline in humanities subjects at A-level;
- great stress on exam results, targets and individualistic success in schools' policy;
- scarcity of transformative learning courses in initial education;

- reliance on a small number of token pilots and temporary projects for community and family learning.

All these indicate that if all the relevant learning as defined in Chapter 1 could be plotted as in Figure 8.3, the content of particular individual learning projects and strategies would be seen to be drawn consistently towards the work-related apex, and that overall they would cluster fairly close to that corner. Community learning would show up as severely neglected; and personal/family developmental learning would also be seen to be poorly subscribed, particularly by younger age groups. The whole array of learning, in fact, would be shown to be strongly biased towards the economic, and the more so as people feel a sense of economic risk spreading across the social order.

If this is indeed what is happening, it would show that – despite a weak signalling of skill needs by employers – people are nevertheless striving hard to find safe economic ground to achieve the lifestyles which the economic system, with great ingenuity, offers them. The middle classes cannot automatically rely on the social position of their parents to underpin their own living standards. What they aim for now is a demonstration of merit and position.

Learning paradoxes
Yet here is the paradox. People strain to meet the employers' needs by showing merit; but the motivation needed to show such merit, in the academically biased world of education, is unsuited to the task of pushing UK Limited upmarket in a vastly competitive world economic environment. What a national workforce needs for this

includes:
- high levels of intrinsic motivation to learn;[16]
- sharing of knowledge and skill in teams;[17]
- thirst for creativity;
- acceptance of risk;
- long-term perspectives;
- commitment to sustainability.[18]

These are aspects of motivation which, despite flurries of rhetoric, are not high-lighted in official educational policy. The very qualifications which so many people still see as the passport for success are already on the trailing edge. Our institutions might as well be teaching Pitman shorthand and the use of the slide-rule. As a result, people strain to offer what employers want the least.

A second paradox lies behind the first. Even if the true needs of the employers were to be addressed by themselves, they would only succeed in speeding up the carousel of economic globalization, thereby deepening the commodification process that under-mines family, community generativity and futurity; destroying the nursery of learning motivation; destabilising personal identity, and increasing apocalyptic angst.

These are the binds which are the funda-mental challenge. As far as learning goes, this is where the true significance of cradle-to-grave lifelong learning strategies is to be found. We have argued elsewhere that a necessary part of any solution to the uncontrolled rampage of globalization is to develop a motivation for cradle-to-grave lifelong learning.[19] This would be of a kind to balance the narrow agenda of individuals' commitment to economic survival and avoiding social exclusion, with a broader involvement in learning for social, family and personal developmental purpose. Such motivation would reposition the centre of gravity of learning benefit closer to the centre of the triangle in Figure 8.3.

This is the perspective we adopt below in considering motivational strategy. The proposition is that, according to all available indications, the cat's cradle currently produces a bias, resulting in an excessive and self-defeating dependence on poorly targeted, economic learning; and that this does not break the grip of postmodern dynamics, but only serves to tighten it. Government and other stakeholders will have to manipulate the cat's cradle into a dy-namic balance favouring cradle-to-grave lifelong learning, based on the twin pillars of individual and social commitment. Only if this is done will the criterion of minimizing the regret in people's lives really be addressed.

Government is, of course, itself inside the force field, skewing the balance of learning, and so is subject to pressure from every kind of interest and lobby group. While it will need to work with other influencers and be fully aware of their interests, it can only succeed on the basis that it is demo-cratically accountable to the electorate for a motivational strategy – one which says what it means, and means what it says; and which does not try to be all things to all people.

Changing a population's general level and mix of learning motivation entails culture change. It is a task for the long-haul – a couple of decades at least. Government would need to form an unequivocal view of learning motivation, and seek to have it progressively endorsed by the electorate. In the area of motivation, above all, the last thing needed is authoritarian government in a hurry to impose its will.

Towards a long-term motivational strategy

The cat's cradle of influence could be reshaped by a number of strategic moves. What would these look like? And has any one of them the capacity by itself to achieve the necessary balance?

Possible strategies

Market forces and efficiency: This aims to support every influencer to increase the efficiency of what they individually want to do, producing more and better directed effort in the cat's cradle overall. This would be done by improving meta-knowledge of motivation, and by coaching improved assessment skills and strategy formulation for all comers – individuals, teachers, institutions, groups, and employers. Compared to the current situation, there would be a new activity in motivational matters, involving deeper consideration of goals and personal capacity, and fewer tired clichés in identifying value.

Supply side: This leaves the solution to suppliers, by sustaining learners' motivation during the learning process and its coping and reflective stages; improving learning products and supporting services, and matching them closely to motivations and strategies held by other parties; and by restructuring those motivations and strategies by persuasion and attitude change. This covers a lot of ground, ranging from teacher morale on the one hand to advertising on the other – taking in issues like second-best learning choices, qualifications, and the curriculum on the way. It is surprising how

little motivational thinking has been done on the supply side in the past.[20] The inflexibility and lack of client sensitivity speaks of a hairshirt educational culture, largely propped up by backdoor funding from government.

In a new approach, suppliers and their funders would have to make most of the running in seeking improvement. For some aspects they would use market intermediaries, such as the University for Industry, to supply motivating portals. Free-standing information and guidance providers would also have a larger role in assisting clients with their project goals and their longer term learning strategies, through an ongoing, supportive relationship – rather like the general practitioner's role in medicine.

The specific skills agenda: This approach would mean that employers take the competitiveness issue more seriously, assess their skill needs better, and signal these needs more clearly and generously to would-be learners inside employment or in the open labour market. It would rely on better extrinsic motivation for skills learning, spread through more effective markets, rather than become involved in identity-based worker development schemes and learning organisations. This approach is likely to favour high-level, scarce skills, and to redistribute income to the people who have them. At the same time it promises more income, and more jobs at basic entry level, such as in call-centres.

People with very high skills would identify and win the business; the business itself would be pursued mainly by workers with a fairly high minimum standard for labour market entry, but with limited chances of rising to the top (so-called operatives).

While a few, very talented people will receive exceptional remuneration at international pay levels, most people in work are likely to have pay rates pegged down by the availability of growing supplies of equally, or more highly, skilled people working for much lower wages anywhere else in the world. It will not be very interesting for them and the incentive for economic learning among people in excluded sectors of the population would remain low, because the entry step would be large, and because the margin of new jobs is small, unstable and poorly paid.

A social learning agenda: Combining family learning, community learning, and social learning support from the employers:

• For families, this agenda would help family groups to formulate and press their own learning needs, particularly in non-economic and social aspects of living. It would assist with parenting skills and morale; and would involve the wider family as an expression of generativity.

• For communities, it would provide policies that decentralise responsibilities, stimulate social awareness, and improve the capacity of communities to organise collectively for the purpose of problem solving through learning. This stronger current of collective action needs to run within groups; but also across groups, within a concept of community overall.[21]

• In the workplace, it would encourage employers to shift towards sustainability, more ethical production and responsible marketing; the creation of identity-based, learning organisations amongst the workforce;[22] the promotion of work-family

balance; social responsibility for employers' impact on local communities; and greater involvement by workers in the making of company decisions. This would begin to position the employer to address the longer term issues of sustainability, and in particular the need to sustain viable families and communities. These are, after all, the infrastructure of generativity, trust and stability without which the whole economic model will eventually stymie.

Redistribution in the field of learning: This relies on government taxing the population at large, and supplying free or cheaper learning opportunities to motivate those who find learning too costly or difficult to arrange. This is the access approach to learning promotion. It works around the margins of social exclusion, and seeks to put a floor into learning motivation. Attention centres on those inescapably set in motivational deficit, while the vast bulk of the population is left to get on with its own motivation and strategies. Instead of strategies which offer something for most people, it is a worst-first solution. It is left to choice whether the purpose is for the deprived to shake off their oppression by capitalistic forces or by higher social power structures, through critical learning, as Paulo Freire would have it;[23] or whether it is a lifeboat function, seeking to pull those who otherwise would drown into the boat of learning success.

Compulsion: Taking the approach of compulsion, government obliges more people to learn in approved areas of study or practice, through raising the compulsory school leaving age or forcing the updating of skills in professional or occupational areas; or it may oblige stakeholders, such as employers or learning providers, to offer learning opportunities which they would not otherwise offer. It may do such things because it wishes to control the content and amount of learning directly, rather than seeking to motivate people to choose to learn content which is primarily in the long term public interest, or to motivate stakeholders to offer it. One reason might be a declared inability to motivate individuals to be sufficiently public spirited; or a despair that employers can actually motivate people through the labour market to acquire the skills which are needed.

Which strategy?

Most of these strategic moves would make some useful contribution to the motivational rebalancing which, by the arguments above, should be our aim. None of them seems remotely sufficient by itself to accomplish the task.

Market forces and efficiency: Raising motivational efficiency all round might increase the effort pulling hither and thither in the cat's cradle of motivational influence. But it is fundamentally unclear that this would change the balance of forces, or address the issue of bias in learning outputs overall.

Supply side: Supply side improvement has real advantages, but on a broad assessment it would be unrealistic to assume that inhibition – due to poor family and community experience, low social support, budget unfeasibility and high cost, and the distractive power of alternatives – can all be set aside by well targeted learning supply. By itself supply side improvement is unlikely to shift the bias in outputs to any large extent.

This is partly because much supply of learning is commercial, and there is little reason

to think that commercial activity to develop client numbers through advertising, outreach and the like, would shift the downbeat motivational assessments underlying much of the demand in weak areas like community and family learning. Maximising profit is unlikely to push suppliers into these difficult markets, away from fashionable web based economic learning. Even if it did, the impediments to learning run far wider than issues which can be remedied by attributes of supply. In part it is also a question of the impact of public funding. The allocation of funding direct to institutions, rather than through the spending of individual learners, feeds a deep culture of producer sovereignty, wrapped up in a patch-and-mend financial stringency. Until this is reformed the relative neglect of motivational outreach will continue.

Specific skills agenda: This is central to any consideration of learning motivation, and has benefits which no policy could afford to ignore. But there are also long-term, bad, side-effects, which need to be offset against the benefits. It does little to allay the disruption of families and the blasting of communities by consumption. It may even make them worse. Moreover, the pyramid of skills would probably continue stretching up to higher and higher levels, with the proportions of intermediate skills narrowing, and the general mimumum entry level of skill for the employed labour force rising sharply. By itself, this is a recipe for deeper social exclusion. Those people trapped in it find escape more difficult; and if employed people do not raise their level of skill, they fall out of contention. It also raises the long-term issue of the discouragement and demotivation of the entry level workers themselves, many of whom may be well qualified, but are lacking in real opportunity to advance and thrive in modern flat corporate structures. In essence, this skills centred policy would cream off the nation's talent, in much the same way as in athletics super-athletes are selected from the normal system and given extra coaching to win Olympic medals, without improving provision for the rest.

The social learning agenda: Has a direct and central role to play in correcting imbalance in the profile of learning and offsetting the problems in the skills agenda. The three interlocking areas of social learning policy have the potential to release more productive energies and creativity, and more efficiency and flexibility, than the skill centred approach ever could by itself.

If pursued exclusively, its central weakness would be a neglect of the bread-and-butter issues of income and jobs. We have seen how lack of resources in families and communities can induce deep fatalism about the chances of successful learning; and how tightness of resources causes serious strains on the time budgets and internal organisation of families – reducing the social capital and altruism available for learning, shortening time horizons, and strangling self-esteem. Although it does not follow that raising resources is sufficient to put all these things right, if significant progress is to be made it is probably necessary. So no one can duck the question of how an individual and a family can get a decent income and working conditions to underpin effective living and learning.

There is here a central bind for motivational policy: more income is needed to bolster the motivation to learn, particularly in ways which are related to family and community. Yet the invasive implications of employment – on its prevailing terms of flexible working, long hours and stress – are to weaken motivations for learning other than the economic. Income adds scope, but employment denies it. The employers' part of the social agenda addresses this directly. It offers ways of so improving efficiency that family and community-friendly employment policies can be put in place to soften the adverse impact of earning a living.

Redistribution: Is bound to play an essential part in healing the motivational split in the population against those from poor social backgrounds with no track record of successful learning. But a whole strategy cannot be based on this alone. Politicians would have difficulty in obtaining voters' consent for a grand redistributive strategy, because the majority have many learning issues of their own, and would have to lose out in order to finance the redistribution. Although problems of family and community learning are particularly acute in low income areas, they actually run across most, if not all, social groups and localities in one significant form or another. If impoverished areas and groups were targeted there would still be huge numbers of non-deprived people who are second-besting, demoralised, and misdirected in their learning. Moreover, extending a ladder of resources down into the deeper recesses of social exclusion begs the question whether people will actually be motivated to climb up to learn, and then whether that new learning will have the balance needed in the public interest.

Compulsion: Destroys self-esteem, buries motivational issues, and distorts priorities. It introduces power play into what needs to be done with consent, and it raises funda-mental difficulties about what content of learning the authorities will choose to enforce. It cannot by definition overcome any bias in motivational processes because it tries to step round them. In doing so, it is likely to make motivational issues worse and not better.

A mixed solution

This suggests strongly that the UK should adopt an across the board approach, draw-ing flexibly on these approaches, barring compulsion. The key aim would be to pre-vent a swamping of learning by economic interests, and to help people to learn much more in personal, family and social dimen-sions as well. Provided that this corrective slant can be applied by means of public pol-icy, ratified, as it should be, by democratic consent, all the approaches listed (barring compulsion) can be applied in concert, with all the motivation that can be mustered amongst the motivators. This would make full use of the complementarity available, and use the social economy option to enhance the effectiveness of the skills approach and compensate for its adverse social side effects. Such a strategy would be a clear rejection of the doctrine that it does not matter what the learning is as long as there is more of it.

This broad, mixed motivational strategy would support the emergence of a new cul-ture of lifelong learning, where individuals are constantly seeking to learn, and exhibit both individual commitment to learn for personal reasons, but also a social commit-ment towards mutual learning in the wider social context, including the world of work. At the heart of the latter is the notion of social capital as applied to learning. Learning

which is undertaken jointly between people, with an element of mutual support, not only creates specific knowledge, it builds social capital as well. This can underpin more learning, and serve wider social purposes as well. Purely individualistic learning strategies, like the individual commitment strategies of the former Conservative Government, miss this central point.

This many-sided strategy would have to be supported by motivational monitoring and evaluation through direct, properly designed, motivational surveys.[24] These are perfectly feasible, although they do raise many issues of methodology. The potential has been explored in a study and seminar supported by the University for Industry. It is high time for statistical practice to make strides in this area.

The key

At the start of this book we set out to show that the levels of motivation displayed by individuals reflects their personal experience; that every healthy person has the potential for high levels of learning motivation; and that there are a host of practical steps that can be taken to improve motivation for learning across the population. The chapters on motiva-tional processes, and on how motivation is influenced, bear out all three propositions. The potential they embody can only be realised by a sound national motivational learning strategy, led by a government which is clear about its intentions; has effec-tive arrangements to conduct the research, and to gather the motivational data; wins proper consent for the strategy, and establishes its effectiveness in practice. Suggestions for the strategy are set out in the Agenda for Action.

Notes and references (Numbers refer to publications listed in the Reference section)

[1] See Beck 19; also 20, 86, 99, 126 & 178.

[2] For such as there is, see 21, 161, 177, 184; see also 250 for a review of material.

[3] On the grounds of length, we have resisted the temptation to distinguish between globalization and post-modernity (or 'late modernity', as in Giddens 99). We see globalization as the economic face of post-modernity, the cultural phenomenon.

[4] Social exclusion takes over from the class-based concept of the proletariat. See Jordan 149 for an analysis of clubs; also 36.

[5] See Ashton & Green 8.

[6] See Gallie et al 95 for an important analysis of employment change.

[7] See 86.

[8] See Beck 19.

[9] See 145.

[10] See Sargant 206.

[11] See 25.

[12] See Bentley 23 for the possibilities here; also 5, 13, 49.

[13] See Folley 91; also Smith & Spurling 222, 230.

[14] For these three categories see 221, 222 & 223.

[15] See 21.

[16] See Csikszentmihalyi 53 & 54 on flow and creativity; also 130.

[17] See Poell et al 194; also 81 & 131.

[18] See Beck 19.

[19] See 220.

[20] See 250 for a summary discussion of supply-side possibilities.

[21] Clark 41 has articulated this well.

[22] Employee development schemes would be involved here. See 17.

[23] See 90.

[24] See 250.

Agenda for action

The final step is to consider what measures might make up the mixed strategy to be pursued. The following agenda sets out main suggestions under key headings – some measures being relevant to more than one heading. This is not an exhaustive list of possibilities. More detail appears in the authors' research reports for the Esmée Fairbairn Foundation, the Talent Foundation, and Ufi Ltd.

Motivational efficiency in the market

- Learning provider organisations to prepare wide ranging motivational strategies. This should be a requirement for all publicly funded bodies, and a key aspect of quality assurance.

- Improved qualification structures with units and full credit accumulation and transfer. Provision of a national database for learning achievements.

- Subsidized courses for learners on enhancing their motivation; motivational support and coaching facilities for learners; and widespread supply of transformative and critical learning opportunities.

- Subsidized lifelong guidance facilities for would-be learners, acting as intermediaries in the learning market.

- Coaching and information on motivation for parents and senior family members, to help them to articulate and satisfy motivation for family learning.

- Encouragement of specialist social entrepreneurs to promote awareness of the opportunities for community-based learning, and to find ways to pool resources and motivation to address them effectively on a permanent basis.

- A legal requirement on every employing organisation to prepare a learning strategy, according to a simple Code of Practice. This aims to strengthen the connection between product market opportunities and the motivational signals given to internal and external labour markets. This would go well beyond the current, still rather narrow, Investors in People approach.

- Rights for employees to receive, as part of their employment contracts, clear information about their rights to training and time off, the rewards of learning, and about the financial and administrative conventions (rules of the game).

- Each employee to have a right to a regular needs assessment jointly with the employer, and to have a personal record of all significant certificated and uncertificated learning, which is standardised and travels with the worker throughout employment anywhere.

• Government to review the possibility of establishing clearer conventions for distributing the burden of arranging and funding learning programmes in employment, and for individuals, families and communities.

• Provision of a comprehensive, integrated system of lifelong learning accounts, with the three key functions – save, borrow and credit. These would support both learning and guidance. Do this in a partnership between local and national government, employers, charities, trades unions, banks and financial institutions.

• Government to commit to funding an independent learning promotional authority which would exercise a broad remit to promote generic learning to the whole UK population, and fund programmes of outreach to particular deprived groups and areas. The funding would be substantial (at least £25m per annum), and would be guaranteed for the long run. A large proportion of the funding would be recouped from suppliers. A proper promotional strategy would be needed, based on comprehensive research of motivational profiles of the population and of cultural and attitudinal change.

Supply
• Respond to the needs of families, communities and employers under the social learning initiatives.

• Learning suppliers to follow the principles and practice of identity-centred learning organisations in their own teaching, research and mentoring activities.

• Better pay, conditions and time for teachers to motivate them to pass on their love of learning more effectively, and to maintain themselves as active lifelong learners.

• Supply to be increasingly funded over the counter via individual learning accounts rather than institutional per capita funding and special bidding. This will help to promote sensitivity to individuals' motivation, and also foster learner commitment.

• Detailed motivational research by new style surveys into product and service improvement, second-preferencing among learners, better teaching methods, support in coping, etc.

• Improved client assurance through abolition of up front fees, ending minimum class size rules, money back guarantees, and insurance provision against withdrawal from learning etc.

• New facilities for helping learners to reflect on their recently completed learning.

• Extended use of group formation and socialising practices to establish the best conditions for shared learning. This influencing of class membership and peer groupings is important for social capital.

• Abandonment of the paternalistic hairshirt view of institutionalised learning, and replacement of it with a new, fully monitored, interest in intrinsic motivation, flow, and conducive learning environments.

• General mentoring schemes on offer for all learners, as a source of direct influence and as social capital.

• Reform the National Curriculum to support motivational development of children, and require all pupils in state funded education to have individual learning plans agreed with the pupils and the parents, with individual (non-comparative) running performance assessment against them, and proper facilities for coping support.

• Avoid damaging instructional methods in initial education, such as open intelligence testing, or excessive competition between learners, or unhelpful social comparison of learning achievement.

Specific skill needs
• Each employee to receive motivational awareness training and to have access to motivational coaching and transformative learning, and to independent guidance services.

• Support for managers' activities in helping to motivate workers to improve their skills and then to apply them fruitfully. Courses on motivation, and development of motivational coaching skills.

• Outreach workers and guidance workers in the community to link excluded or economically inactive people better to the opportunities in the labour market.

• Legislation outlawing age discrimination in the labour market and in employment.

• Clear updating requirements, analogous to those being introduced in the medical profession, for all vocational qualifications.

• Individual lifelong learning accounts to be used universally in support of skills related learning, collecting spendable (and sometimes conditional) funds for skills learning from employers, trade

unions, government, and other sources. This will bring personal autonomy to bear, and augment resources for skills investment.

• Use of lifelong learning accounts system to recover employers' training investments lost through labour mobility and poaching.

Social learning agenda: families, communities and workplaces

Families
• Recognition in housing, social and educational policies of the need for non-chaotic and supportive learning environments for the whole learning family, both inside and outside the home.

• Recognition in parenting courses of the importance of effective parenting, and of approaches for strengthening motivation.

• Support for dysfunctional families, where parental efficacy is reduced to danger levels. Special coaching services available in learning institutions to address low motivation among young people.

• Development of the concept of the family as an identity-based, intergenerational, learning organisation. Good practice case studies and materials, and public badges of recognition.

• Development of the lifelong learning account concept within the extended family, in order to give expression to cross-generational interest in the promotion of learning.

• Direct financial support for family learning in socially excluded populations through lifelong learning accounts and family learning guidance facilities.

• Encouragement of circles of learning families to establish supportive social capital outside the home.

• Close communication and even-handed co-operation between schools and families over the needs of children, what the school should do, what roles family members can play, and the support which will enable them to do so.

Communities
• Far greater efforts towards the development of pro-social values in initial education, and in community and family learning.

• Action to establish peer-group social capital between organisations and schemes which are involved in community-related learning.

• Encouraging learning as a part of identity-based community groups, e.g. ethnic communities to research and teach their own traditions and cultural contributions within and beyond their own communities.

• Developing the national learning account system to create a demand for targeted community learning, and to establish long term funding instead of the impermanent and debilitating bid-culture, where groups compete against each other for an uncertain share of short term and experimental project budgets.

• Good practice guidance for community projects involving learning, recognising the differences between initial capacity building projects, and projects which directly address community needs.

• Support research into informal social networks, and their key shakers and movers,

to establish how they can best be used to support the demand for community-related learning.

Workplaces
• General establishment of worker development schemes (on the EDAP model pioneered by Ford Motors). These encourage social capital between worker-learners, irrespective of grade or function, and act to build corporate identity-based learning organisations in or around the workplace.

• Laws to restrict excessive hours, and to grant workers periodic time-off for study, in lieu of any excessive hours worked.

• Encouragement for workers to take time off for help in family-related or community-related learning activities.

• Job enrichment and improved job satisfaction for standard operatives.

• Worker mentoring schemes, to build social capital on the shop floor, with training in informal encouragement and guidance (of the kind often supplied by Ford EDAP advisers and some shop floor union officials).

• Encouragement for the voluntary establishment of learning organisation policies in the workplace, supported by a Super Investors in People standard. Publication of advice and case studies by government.

• Encouragement of mutual support between employers on the practice of learning organisation policies, and on family and community-related activities. This will build organisational social capital in support of learning motivation across domains.

General tax relief for company expenditures in these areas.

• Development of a new Code of Practice for product design and marketing, which will raise and highlight the learning value of products and services.

• Relaxation of employment entry skill standards for would-be workers who have suffered from social exclusion. This will build on the New Deal, and counter the continuing upward drift in basic skill requirements.

Redistribution

• Redistribute public funding of learning post compulsory schooling through the learning accounts, to target support on family and community issues, and to tackle the problems of social exclusion and the low participation in post-compulsory learning of disadvantaged and deprived social groups.

• Make all basic entitlements to public funding for education flexible, in terms of time and mode. This can be achieved through a national system of learning accounts.

• Reform the admissions arrangements to all publicly funded educational institutions to establish, as far as possible, a balanced social entry, and to resist calls for more specialised streaming within schools.

References

Items marked ** are recommended for general reading

1. Abrams, D & Hogg, M eds (1999) *Social Identity and Social Cognition*. Oxford: Blackwell **

2. Adam, B (1990) *Time and Social Theory*. Cambridge: Polity Press

3. Adams, G ed (2000) *Adolescent Development Essential Readings*. Oxford: Blackwell

4. Admiraal, W & Korthagen, F & Wubbels, T (2000) *Effects of student teachers' coping behaviour*. British Journal of Educational Psychology 70: 33-52

5. Alexander, T & Clyne, P (1995) *Riches beyond Price*. Leicester: NIACE

6. Alwin, D (1994) *Ageing, personality and social change. The stability of individual differences over the adult life span*. in 84

7. Apple, M (1996) *Cultural Politics and Education*. Buckingham: Open University Press

8. Ashton, D & Green, F (1996) *Education, Training and the Global Economy*. Cheltenham: Edward Elgar **

9. Bandura, A (1986) *Social Foundations of Thought and Action*. Englewood Cliffs: Prentice Hall **

10. Bandura, A ed (1995) *Self Efficacy in Changing Societies*. Cambridge: Cambridge University Press

11. Bandura, A (1997) *Self Efficacy: The Exercise of Control*. New York: W H Freeman & Co

12. Barnett, R (1997) *Higher Education: a critical business*. Buckingham: Society for Research into Higher Education/ OU Press **

13. Bastiani, J (1997) *Home-School Work in Multicultural Settings*. London: Fulton

14. Barg, J (1990) *Auto-motives: Preconscious Determinants of Social Interaction*. In 137

15. Baron, R & Kerr, N & Miller, M (1992) *Group Processes, Group Decision, Group Action*. Buckingham: Open University Press **

16. Beach, S & Tesser, A (1995) *Self esteem and the extended self-evaluation maintenance model: the self in social context*. In 155

17. Beattie, A (1997) *Working People and Lifelong Learning: a study of the impact of an employee development scheme*. Leicester: NIACE

18. Beck, J (1998) *Morality and Citzenship in Education*. London: Cassell

19. Beck, U (1992) *Risk Society*. London: Sage

20. Beck, U & Giddens, A & Lash, S (1994) *Reflexive Modernization*. Oxford: Polity Press/ Blackwell **

21. Beinart, S & Smith, P (1997) *National Adult Learning Survey*. London: DfEE

22. Bennett, R & Glennester, H & Nevison, D (1993) *Learning Should Pay*. London: BP Education Services and LSE

23. Bentley, T (1999) *Learning beyond the Classroom*. London: Demos

24. Bergin, D (1995) *Effects of a Mastery Versus Competitive Situation on Learning*. Journal of Experimental Education 63 (4): 303-314

25. Blatchford, P (1998) *The state of play in schools*. Child Psychology and Psychiatry Review Vol 3 No 2: 58-67

26. Blundell, R & Deerden, L & Goodman A, & Reed H (1997) *Higher Education, Employment and Earnings in Britain*. London: Institute of Fiscal Studies

27. Blundell, R & Dearden, L & Meghir, C (1996) *The Determinants and Effects of Work-related Training in Britain*. London: Institute of Fiscal Studies

28. Bondy, E & Mash, E (1999) *Parenting efficacy, perceived control over care-giving failure, and mothers' reactions to pre-school children's misbehaviour*. Child Care Journal Vol 29 No 3: 157-173

29. Booth A & Snower D eds (1996) *Acquiring Skills: Market Failures, Their Symptoms and Policy Responses*. Cambridge: Centre for Economic Policy Research **

30. Brandtstadter, J & Rothermund, K & Schmitz, U (1998) *Maintaining self-integrity and efficacy through adulthood and later life. The adaptive functions of assimilative and accommodative flexibility*. In 128

31. Brown, R (2000) *Group Processes (ed.2)*. Oxford: Blackwell **

32. Brown, S & Armstrong, S & Thompson, G (1998) *Motivating Students*. London: Kogan Page

33. Buchanan, J (1965) *An Economic Theory of Clubs*. Economica Feb 1965: 456-469

34. Buechler,S (2000) *Social Movements in Advanced Capitalism*. Oxford: Oxford University Press **

35. Busato,V & Prins, F & Elshout, J & Harnaker, C (1999) *The Relationship Between Learning Style: personality and individual differences*. Elsevier: London

36. Byrne, D (1999) *Social Exclusion*. Buckingham: Open University Press

37. Campbell, M (1995) *Learning Pays: Individual Commitment, Learning and Economic Development*. Leeds: Leeds Metropolitan University

38. Carver, C & Scheier, M (1990) *Principles of Self-Regulation: Action and Emotion*. In 137

39. Caspi, A (1998) *Personality development across the life course*. In 57

40. Chapman, G (1998) *Sooner or later: the psychology of inter temporal choice*. The Psychology of Learning and Motivation Vol 38: 83-113

41. Clark, D (1995) *Schools as Learning Communities*. London: Cassell **

42. Coare, P & Thompson, A (1996) *Through the Joy of Learning*. Leicester: NIACE

43. Coffield, F (1999) *Why's the Beer Always Stronger Up North?* Bristol: Policy Press

44. Coffield, F (1999) *Learning at Work*. Bristol: Policy Press

45. Coffield, F ed (2000) *Differing Visions of a Lifelong Learning Society*. Research Findings Vol 1. Bristol: Policy Press

46. Colquitt, J & Simmering, M (1998) *Conscientiousness, goal orientation, and the motivation to learn during the learning process: a longitudinal study*. Journal of Applied Psychology Vol 83 No 4: 654-665

47. Connell, J & Wellborn, J (1991) *Competence, autonomy and relatedness: a motivational analysis of self-esteem processes*. In 117

48. Coopers & Lybrand (1995) *National Evaluation for Skill Choice*. Sheffield: Coopers & Lybrand

49. Crick, B for the Advisory Group on Citizenship (1998). *Final report - Education for Citizenship and Teaching of Democracy in Schools*. London: QCA/DfEE

50. Crowder, M & Pupynin, K (1993) *The Motivation to Train*. Research Series 9. Sheffield: Employment Department

51. Crowder, M (1995) *Individual Commitment to Learning: understanding motivation - Final Report*. Sheffield:

Employment Department
52. Csikszentmihalyi, M (1996) *Creativity.*
New York: Harper Collins
53. Csikszentmihalyi, M (1997) *Living Well:
the Psychology of Everyday Life.* London:
Phoenix **
54. Csikszentmihalyi, M & Rathunde, K
(1993) *The measurement of flow in everyday
life: toward a theory of emergent motivation.*
Nebraska Symposium on Motivation
Vol 40 Developmental Perspectives in
Motivation: 57-97
55. Damasio, A (2000) *The Feeling of What
Happens.* London: Heinemann **
56. Damasio, A (1994) *Descartes' Error:
Emotion, Reason and the Human Brain.* New
York: Grosset/Putnam
57. Damon, W & Eisenberg, N (1998) *Handbook
of Child Psychology 5th Ed.* Vol 3 Social,
Emotional and Personality Development.
Chichester: John Wiley & Sons **
58. Dearden, L, Machin, S, Reed, H, &
Wilkinson, D (1997) *Labour Turnover and
Work-related Training.* London: Institute for
Fiscal Studies
59. Deci, E (1985) *Why We Do What We Do.*
Harmondsworth: Penguin **
60. Deci, E & Ryan, R (1985) *Intrinsic
Motivation and Self Determination in Human
Behaviour.* London: Plenum Press
61. Deci, E & Ryan, R (1995) *Human
autonomy: the basis for true self-esteem.* In 155
62. Deci, E & Ryan, R & Koestner, R (1999)
*A meta-analytic review of experiments
examining the effects of extrinsic rewards on
intrinsic motivation.* Psychogical Bulletin Vol
125 No 6: 627-668
63. Degenne, A & Forse, M (1999)
Introducing Social Networks. London: Sage
64. Demos (1998) *The Good Life.* London:
Demos
65. Dench, S & Regan, J (2000) *Learning in
Later Life: Motivation and Impact.* DfEE

Research Report RR183. Nottingham: DfEE
66. Digenti, D (1998) *Toward an
Understanding of the Learning Community.*
Organisation Development Journal Vol 16
No 2 Summer 98
67. Dirkx, J (1998) *Transformative learning
theory in the practice of adult education: an
overview.* PAACE Journal of Lifelong
Learning Vol 7: 1-14
68. Dornyei, Z (2000) *Motivation in Action:
Towards a process oriented conceptualisation
of Student Motivation.* British Journal of
Educational Psychology 70, 519-538.
Leicester: British Psychological Society
69. Dweck, C (2000) *Self Theories: Their role
in motivation, personality and development.*
Hove: Taylor & Francis **
70. Eccles, J & Wigfield, A (1995) *In the mind
of the actor: the structure of adolescents'
achievement task values and expectancy-
related beliefs.* Journal of Personality and
Social Psychology Vol 21 No 3: 215-225
71. Eccles, J & Wigfield, A & Schiefle, U
(1998) *Motivation to succeed.* In 57
72. Edwards, R & Hanson, A & Raggatt, P
(1996) *Boundaries of Adult Learning.* London:
Routledge/The Open University
73. Eisenberg, N & Mussen, P (1989) *The
Roots of Pro-social Behaviour in Children.*
Cambridge: Cambridge University Press **
74. Elliot, A & Church, M (1997) *A
hierarchical model of approach and avoidance
achievement motivation.* Journal of
Personality and Social Psychology Vol 72
No 1: 218-232
75. Elliot, A & Sheldon, K (1997) *Avoidance
Achievement Motivation: A personal goals
analysis.* Journal of Personality and Social
Psychology Vol 73 No 1: 171-185
76. Elsdon, K & Reynolds, J & Stewart, S
(1995) *Voluntary Organisation: citizenship,
learning and change.* Leicester: NIACE
77. Epstein, S (1991) *Cognitive-experiential*

self-theory: implications for developmental psychology. In 117

78. Epstein, S & Morling, B (1995) *Is the self motivated to do more than enhance and/or verify itself?* In 155

79. Eraut, M (2000) *Non-formal learning and tacit knowledge in professional work.* British Journal of Educational Psychology 70: 113-136

80. Eraut, M & Alderton, J & Cole, G & Senker, P *Learning from other people at work.* in 44

81. Eraut, M & Alderton, J & Cole, G & Senker, P *Development of Knowledge and Skills at Work.* In 45

82. Falk, I & Harrison, L (1998) *Community Learning and Social Capital: 'Just having a little chat'.* Journal of Vocational Education and Training Vol 50: No 4

83. Fantuzzo, J & Tighe, E & Childs, S (2000) *Family involvement questionnaire: a multivariate assessment of family participation in early childhood education.* Journal of Educational Psychology Vol 92 No 2: 367-376

84. Featherman, D & Learner, R & Perlmutter, M eds (1994) *Life span, Development and Behaviour Vol 12* Hillsdale NJ: Erlbaum **

85. Feather, N (1990) *Bridging the Gap between Values and Actions: Recent Applications of the Expectancy-Value Model.* In 137

86. Featherstone, M (1992) *Culture Theory and Cultural Change.* London: Sage

87. Feinstein, L (1998) *Pre-school educational inequality? British children in the 1970 cohort.* Discussion Papers 382 and 404. London: Centre for Economic Performance LSE

88. Firth, D & Goffey, L (1996) *Individual Commitment: tracking learners' decision making.* DfEE Research Studies RS6. London: HMSO

89. Fiske, J (1987) *Television Culture.* London: Routledge

90. Freire, P (1993) *Pedagogy of the Oppressed.* 2nd edition. London: Penguin **

91. Foley, G (1999) *Learning in Social Action.* Leicester: NIACE

92. Forgas, J ed (2001) *Handbook of Affect and Social Cognition.* London: Erbaum

93. Gallagher, W (1999) *How places affect people.* Architectural Record Feb 1999: 75-82

94. Gallie, D & White, M (1993) *Employee Commitment and the Skills Revolution: first findings.* London: PSI

95. Gallie, D & White, M & Cheng, Y & Tomlinson, M (1998) *Restructuring the Employment Relationship.* Oxford: Clarendon **

96. Gardner, H (1993) *Frames of Mind: the theory of multiple intelligences.* 2nd edition. London: Fontana **

97. Gardner, H (1993) *Multiple Intelligencies: the theory in practice* New York: Basic Books

98. Gardner, H (1999) *Intelligence Reframed.* New York: Basic Books

99. Giddens, A (1991) *Modernity and Self-identity.* Oxford: Polity Press

100. Gjesme, T (1996) *Future time orientation and motivation.* in 101

101. Gjesme, T & Nygard, R (1996) *Advances in Motivation.* Oslo: Scandinavian University Press

102. Gladwell, M (2000) *The Tipping Point.* London: Little, Brown and Company **

103. Goleman, D (1991) *Emotional Intelligence.* London: Bloomsbury **

104. Gollwitzer, P(1996) *The volitional benefits of planning.* in 105

105. Gollwitzer, P & Barg, J eds (1996) *The Psychology of Action.* London: Guilford **

106. Gollwitzer, P & Kirchof, O (1998) *The wilful pursuit of identity.* in 105

107. Gollwitzer, P & Schaal, B (1998) *Metacognition in action: the importance of implementation intentions.* Personality and Social Psychology Review Vol 2 No 2: 124-136

108. Gorard, S & Rees, G & Fevre, R (1999) 'The two dimensions of time: the changing social context of lifelong learning' in Studies in The Education of Adults. Vol.31 No.1. Leicester: NIACE

109. Green, F (1997) Review of Information on the Benefits of Training for Employers. Research Report 7. Norwich: DfEE

110. Greenier, K & Kernis, M & Waschull, S (1995) Not all high or low self-esteem people are the same: theory and research on the stability of self-esteem. In 155

111. Grolnick, W & Kurowski, C & Gurland, S (1999) Family processes and the development of children's self-regulation. Educational Psychologist 34(1): 3-14

112. Gropnik, A & Meltzoff, A & Kuhl, P (1999) The Scientist in the Crib. New York: William Morrow **

113. Graham, S (1998) Social motivation and perceived responsibility in others attributions and behaviour of African American boys labelled as aggressive. In 128

114. Schon, D (1983) The Reflective Practitioner. New York: Basic Books

115. Guest, D & Conway, N (1998) Fairness at Work and the Psychological Contract. London: Institute of Personnel & Development

116. Guest, D & Conway, N (1997) Employee Motivation and the Psychological Contract. London: Institute of Personnel & Development

117. Gunnar, M & Sroufe, L eds (1991) Self Processes and Development: The Minnesota Symposia on Child Psychology Vol 23. Hillsdale NJ: Erlbaum

118. Hall, P (1997) Demos Collection Issue 12. London: Demos

119. Hall, T & Coffey, A & Williamson, H (1999) Self, space and place: youth identities and citizenship. British Journal of Sociology of Education Vol 20 No 4: 501-513

120. Halsey, A & Lauder, H & Brown, P & Stuart Wells, A (1997) Education: Culture, Economy, and Society. Oxford: Oxford University Press **

121. Hand, A. & Gambles, J & Cooper, E (1994) Individual Commitment to Learning: Individuals' Decision-Making about 'Lifetime Learning' Research Series No 42. Sheffield: Employment Department

122. Harris, E (1997) 'From broadcasting to narrow casting: television as a language of possibility for community development in a learning society' in International Journal of Lifelong Education. Vol.16/1: January. London: Taylor and Francis

123. Harris, J (2000) The outcome of parenting: what do we really know? Journal of Personality 68(3): 625-637

124. Harris, J (1995) Where is the child's environment? A group socialization theory of development. Psychological Review Vol 102 No 3: 458-489

125. Harter, S (1998) The development of self-representations. In 57

126. Harvey, D (1990) The Condition of Postmodernity. Oxford: Blackwell **

127. Heckhausen, J (1999) Developmental Regulation in Adulthood. Cambridge: Cambridge University Press **

128. Heckhausen, J & Dweck, C eds. (1998) Motivation and Self-regulation across the Life span. Cambridge: Cambridge University Press **

129. Heckhausen, J & Schulz, R (1998) Developmental regulation in adulthood: selection and compensation via primary and secondary control. In 128

130. Hennessey, B (1999) Intrinsic motivation, affect and creativity. In 201

131. Hertz-Lazarowitz, R & Miller, N eds. (1992) Interaction in Cooperative Groups. Cambridge: Cambridge University Press **

132. Hickman, G & Bartholomae, S &

McKenry, P (2000) *Influence of parenting styles on the adjustment and academic achievement of traditional college freshmen.* Journal of College Student Development Vol 41 No 1: 41-54

133. Higgins, E Tory (1996) *Ideals, oughts, and regulatory focus.* in 105

134. Higgins, E Tory & Silberman, I (1998) *Development of regulatory focus: promotion and prevention as ways of living.* In 128

135. Higgins, E Tory & Kruglanski, A (2000) *Motivational Science: Social and Personality Perspectives.* Hove: Taylor & Francis Psychology Press **

136. Higgins, E Tory & Trope, Y (1990) *Activity Engagement Theory.* In 137

137. Higgins, E Tory & Sorrentino, R (1990) *Handbook of Motivation and Cognition: Foundations of Social Behaviour* Vol 2. London: Guilford Press

138. Hodkinson, P. & Sparkes, A. & Hodkinson, H. (1996) *Triumphs and Tears - Young people, markets, and the transition from school to work.* London: Fulton

139. Hofstede, G (1994) *Cultures and Organisations.* London: Harper Collins

140. Hogg, M & Abrams, D (1988) *Social Identifications.* London: Routledge **

141. Hogg, M & Abrams, D (1993) *Group Motivation.* London: Harvester Wheatsheaf **

142. Hong, Y & Chiu, C & Dweck, C (1995) *Implicit theories of intelligence: reconsidering the role of confidence in achievement motivation.* In 155

143. Howe, M (1997) *IQ in Question.* London: Sage

144. Hoyle, R & Kernis, M & Leary, M & Baldwin, M (1999) *Selfhood: Identity, esteem, regulation.* Boulder, Colorado: Westview Press **

145. International Survey Research (1997) *Organisational Mutation: employee satisfaction in the '90s.* London: International Survey Research

146. Jacoby, L & Kelley, C (1990) *An Episodic View of Motivation: Unconscious Influences on the Memory.* In 137

147. Johnston, D & Johnston, R (1999) *Learning Together and Alone,* 5th Edition. London: Allyn and Bacon **

148. Johnston, H & Klandermans, B (1995) *Social Movements and Culture.* London: UCL Press **

149. Jordan, B (1996) *A Theory of Poverty and Social Exclusion.* Oxford: Polity Press

150. Juvonen, J & Wentzel, K eds (1996) *Social Motivation: Understanding Children's School Adjustment.* Cambridge: Cambridge University Press **

151. Kagan, J (1998) *Galen's Prophesy: Temperament in Human nature.* Boulder, Colorado: Westview Press

152. Kasser, T & Ryan, R (1993) *A dark side of the American dream: correlates of financial success as a central life aspiration.* Journal of Personality and Social Psychology Vol 65 No 2: 410-422

153. Kasser, T & Ryan, R & Zax, M & Sameroff, A (1995) *The relations of maternal and social environments to late adolescents' materialistic and pro-social values.* Developmental Psychology Vol 31 No 6: 907-914

154. Kelly, C & Breinlinger, S (1996) *The Social Psychology of Collective Action.* London: Taylor and Francis **

155. Kernis, M ed (1995) *Efficacy, Agency and Self-esteem.* New York: Plenum **

156. Klandermans, B (1997) *The Social Psychology of Protest.* Oxford: Blackwell

157. Knippenberg, van D (1999) *Social identity and persuasion: reconsidering the role of group membership.* In 1

158. Kuhl, J (1996) *Motivation and volition.* 25th Congress on Motivation and Volition Chap 15: 311-340

159. Kuhl, J & Fuhrmann, A (1998)

Decomposing self-regulation and self-control: the volitional components inventory. In 128

160. Kruglanski, A & Webster, D (2000) *Motivated Closing of the Mind.* In 135

161. La Valle, I & Finch, S (1999) *Pathways in Adult Learning: A follow-up to the National Adult Learning Survey.* Research Report 137. Sheffield: DfEE

162. Lazarus, R (1993) *Coping theory and research: past, present and future.* Psychosomatic Medicine 55: 234-247

163. Leary, M & Baumeister, R (2000) *The nature and function of self-esteem: sociometer theory.* Advances in Experimental Social Psychology Vol 32: 1-62

164. Lewin, K & Dembo, T & Festinger, L & Sears, P (1944) *Level of Aspiration* in J, Hunt ed (1944) *Personality and the behaviour disorders.* New York: Ronald Press

165. Levy-Shiff, R (1999) *Fathers' cognitive appraisals, coping strategies and support resources as correlates of adjustment to parenthood.* Journal of Family Psychology Vol 13 No 4: 554-567

166. Mackintosh, N (1998) *IQ and Human Intelligence.* Oxford: Oxford University Press

167. Magnusson, D ed (1996) *The Life Span Development of Individuals.* Cambridge: Cambridge University Press

168. Maslow, A (1987) *Motivation and Personality 3rd Edition.* New York: Harper Collins

169. Mayer, J (2001) *Emotion, Intelligence, and Emotional Intelligence.* In 92

170. McClelland, D (1987) *Human Motivation.* Cambridge: Cambridge University Press

171. McGivney, V (1999) *Informal Learning in the Community.* Leicester: NIACE

172. McGivney, V (1992) *Motivating Unemployed Adults to Undertake Education and Training: some British & European findings.* Leicester: NIACE

173. Mezirow, J (1991) *Transformative Dimensions of Adult Learning.* San Francisco: Jossey-Bass

174. McMillan, J & Forsyth, D (1991) 'What theories of motivation say about why learners learn' in New Directions for Teaching and Learning. No 45, Spring. New York: Jossey-Bass **

175. Moll, L et al (1995) *Funds of knowledge for teaching in Latino households.* Urban Education Vol 29 No 4: 443-470

176. Mishan, E (1978) *Cost-benefit Analysis.* London: Allen & Unwin

177. MORI (1998) *Attitudes to Learning - Campaign for Learning Survey 1998.* London: Campaign for Learning

178. Munro, D & Schumaker, J & Carr, S eds (1997) *Motivation and Culture.* London: Routledge

179. Niles, F (1995) *Cultural differences in learning motivation and learning strategies: a comparison of overseas and Australian students at an Australian university.* International Journal of Inter-cultural Relations Vol 19 No 3: 369-385

180. Nix. G & Ryan, R & Manly, J & Deci, E (1999) *Revitalisation through Self-regulation: The effects of autonomous and controlled motivation on happiness and vitality.* Journal of Experimental Social Psychology 35: 266-284

181. Olson, M (1971) *The Logic of Collective Action.* London: Harvard

182. Orpen, C (1999) 'The influence of the training environment on trainee motivation and perceived training quality' in International Journal of Training and Development. 3: 1. Oxford: Blackwell

183. Oulton, N (1996) *Work force skills and economic competitiveness.* In 29

184. Park, A (1994) *Individual Commitment to Learning: Individuals' Attitudes.* Research Series No 32. Sheffield: Employment Department

185. Parr, J (2000) *Identity and Education: The Links for Mature Women Students.* Aldershot: Ashgate

186. Parsons, D & Cocks, N & Rowe, V (1998) *The Role of Employee Development Schemes in Increasing Learning at Work.* Research Report 73. Norwich: DfEE

187. Parsons, S & Bynner, J (1998) *Influences on Adult Basic Skills.* London: Basic Skills Agency

188. Patrick, B & Skinner, E & Connell, J (1993) *What motivates children's behaviour and emotion? Joint effects of perceived control and autonomy in the academic domain.* Journal of Personality and Social Psychology Vol 65 No 4: 781-791

189. Payne, J & Payne, C & Lissenburgh, S & Range, M (1999) *Work-based Training and Job Prospects for the Unemployed: an Evaluation of Training for Work.* Sudbury: DfEE

190. Peterson, C & Maier, S & Seligman, M (1993) *Learned Helplessness.* Oxford: Oxford University Press

191. Pilkington, C & Smith, K (2000) *Self-evaluation maintenance in a larger social context.* British Journal of Social Psychology 39: 213-227

192. Pintrich, P & Marx, R & Boyle, R (1993) *Beyond cold conceptual change: the role of motivational beliefs and class room contextual factors in the process of conceptual change.* Review of Educational Research Vol 63 No 2: 167-199

193. Pintrich, P & Schunk, D (1996) *Motivation and Education.* New Jersey: Prentice Hall-Merrill **

194. Poell, R, van der Krogt, F & Wildersmeersch, D (1998) *Solving work-related problems through learning projects.* International Journal of Lifelong Education. London: Taylor & Francis

195. Psacharopoulos, P (1994) *'Returns to investment in education: a global update'* in World Development. Vol 22 No 9. London: Elsevier

196. Ranson, S. (1998) *Inside the Learning Society.* London: Cassell

197. Reay, D & Wiliam, D (1999) *'I'll be a nothing': structure, agency and the construction of identity through assessment.* British Education Research Journal Vol 25 No 3: 343-354

198. Reber, A (1997) *Implicit ruminations.* Psychonomic Bull. and Review 4(1): 49-55

199. Reed, D (1997) *Following Kolberg.* Notre Dame: University of Notre Dame

200. Rose, C & Nicholl, M (1997) *Accelerated Learning for the 21st Century.* London: Piatkus

201. Russ, S ed (1999) *Affect, Creative Experience, Psychological Adjustment.* London: Brunner Mazel **

202. Ryan, R & Deci, E (2000) *Self determination theory and the facilitation of intrinsic motivation, social development and well being.* American Psychologist Vol 55 No 1: 68-78 **

203. Ryan, R & Kuhl, J & Deci, E (1997) *Nature and autonomy: an organizational view of social and neurobiological aspects of self-regulation in behaviour and development.* Development and Psychopathology Vol 9: 701-728

204. Ryan, R & Sheldon, K & Kasser, T & Deci, E (1996) *All goals are not created equal: an organismic perspective on the nature of goals and regulation.* In 105

205. Ryan, R & Stiller, J & Lynch, J (1994) *Representations of relationships to teachers, parents, and friends as predictors of academic motivation and self-esteem.* Journal of Early Adolescence Vol 14 No 2: 226-249

206. Sargant, N (1997) *The Learning Divide: a study of participation in adult learning in the United Kingdom.* Leicester: NIACE **

207. Sargant, N (1999) *Marking Time: The*

NIACE Survey on Adult Participation.
Leicester: NIACE

208. Schuller, T & Burns, A (1999) *'Using social capital to compare performance in continuing education'.* In 43

209. Schuller, T (1999) *'Exploiting social capital about learning',* unpublished inaugural lecture, Birkbeck College, London

210. Schroeder, D & Penner, L & Dovidio, J & Piliavin, J (1995) *The Psychology of Helping.* London: McGraw-Hill **

211. Seltzer, M & Ryff, C (1994) *Parenting across the life span: the normative and non-normative cases.* In 84

212. Skinner, E (1991) *Development and perceived control: a dynamic model of action in context.* in 117

213. Skinner, E (1995) *Perceived Control, Motivation and Coping.* London: Sage **

214. Skinner, E & Wellborne, J (1994) *Coping during childhood and adolescence: a motivational perspective.* In 84

215. Shah, J & Higgins, E Tory (1997) *Expectancy X Value effects Regulatory Focus and Determinants of Magnitude and Direction.* Journal of Personality and Social Psychology Vol 73 No 5: 447-458

216. Sheldon, K & Elliot, A (1999) *Goal striving, need satisfaction, and longitudinal well-being: the self concordance model.* Journal of Personality and Social Psychology Vol 76 No 3: 482-497

217. Sheldon, K & Ryan, R & Rawsthorne, L & Ilardi, B (1997) *Trait self and true self: cross-role variation in the Big Five personality traits and their relations with psychological authenticity and subjective well-being.* Journal of Personality and Social Psychology Vol 73 No 6: 1380-1393

218. Slavin, R (1983) *Co-operative Learning Second Edition.* London: Allyn and Bacon

219. Smith, C & Kirby, L (2001) *Affect and Cognitive Appraisal Processes.* In 92

220. Smith, J & Spurling, A (1999) *Lifelong Learning: Riding the Tiger.* London: Cassell **

221. Smith, J & Spurling, A (1999) *Learning for work: a study in motivation.* London: Talent Foundation

222. Smith, J & Spurling, A (2000) *Motivation for Community-related Learning: Why Bother?* Bamford: Bamford Taggs Ltd

223. Smith, J & Spurling, A (2000) *Motivation for Developmental Learning: The Individual and the Family.* Bamford: Bamford Taggs Ltd

224. Soucy, N & Lavose, S (2000) *Attachment and control in family and mentoring contexts as determinants of adolescent adjustment to college.* Journal of Family Psychology Vol 14 No 1: 125-143

225. Sorrentino, R & Bobocel, D & Gitta, M & Olson, J (2000) *Uncertainty Orientation and Persuasion.* In 135

226. Sternberg, R (1998) *A balance theory of wisdom.* Review of General Psychology Vol 2 No 4: 347-365

227. Spilsbury, M & Moralee, J & Hillage, J & Frost, D (1995) *Evaluation of the Investors in People in England and Wales, 1994-95.* Falmer: Institute of Employment Studies

228. Stevens, M (1996) *'Transferable training and poaching externalities.'* In 29

229. Stipek, D (1998) *Motivation to Learn.* 3rd edition. London: Allyn & Bacon **

230. Tam, H (1998) *Communitarianism.* London: McMillan

231. Terry, B & Hogg, M & Duck, J (1999) *Group membership, social identity and attitudes.* In 1

232. Tuijnman, A & Van Der Kamp, M ed (1992) *Learning across the life span: theories, research, policies.* Oxford: Pergamon Press **

233. Triandis, H (1995) *Individualism and Collectivism.* Oxford: Westview Press **

234. Usher, R & Edwards, R (1994) *Postmodernism and Education.* London: Routledge

235. Utman, C (1997) *Performance effects of motivational state: a meta-analysis.* Personality and Social Psychology Review Vol 1 No 2: 170-182

236. Vygotsky, L (1978) *Mind in Society: the development of higher psychological processes.* Cambridge, MA: Harvard University Press

237. Wade, B & Moore, M (2000) *A Sure Start with books.* Early Years Vol 20 No 2: 39-46

238. Watson, T (1996) *'Motivation: That's Maslow isn't it?'* in Management Learning, Vol.27 No.4. London: Sage

239. Weinberger, J & McClelland, D (1990) *Cognitive versus Traditional Motivational Models.* In 137

240. Weiner, B (1995) *Judgements of responsibility: a foundation for a theory of social conduct.* London: Guilford

241. Weiner, B (1992) *Human motivation: metaphors, theories and research.* London: Sage **

242. Westby, E & Dawson, V (1995) *Creativity: asset or burden in the classroom.* Creativity Research Journal Vol 8 No 1: 1-10

243. White, H (2000) *Relationship of family socialisation processes to adolescent moral thought.* Journal of Social Psychology 140 (1): 75-91

244. Wicklund, R & Gollwitzer, P (1982) *Symbolic Self-completion.* London: Erlbaum

245. Wilkinson, H ed (2000) *Family Business.* London: Demos

246. Williamson, B (1998) *Lifeworlds and Learning.* Leicester: NIACE

247. Wigfield, A & Eccles, J (2000) *Expectancy-Value Theory of Achievement Motivation* Contemporary Educational Psychology 25: 68-81 **

248. Wood, H & Wood, D (1999) *Help seeking, learning and contingent tutoring.* Computers and Education 33: 153-169

249. Zander, A (1996) *Motives and Goals in Groups.* London: Transaction Publishers

250. Smith, J, & Spurling, A (2000) *Improving Surveys of Motivation for Lifelong Learning.* Unpublished paper for University for Industry